Zen of Zinn

Instant Wisdom from Silicon Valley's
Longest Serving CEO

by Ray Zinn

ISBN: 978-0-692-06861-8

e-ISBN: 978-0-692-06862-5

Library of Congress Cataloging-in-Publication Data
Zinn, Ray.

Zen of Zinn: Instant Wisdom from Silicon Valley's Longest Serving CEO / Ray Zinn.

978-0-692-06861-8

1. Leadership. 2. Culture. 3. Entrepreneurship.

I will be forever grateful to my parents, Pauline and Milton Zinn who raised me with the social graces that have led me throughout my life.

And to my grandfather, Dolpha Lee Zinn, who was called Doc Zinn because he was the town philosopher and people sought him out for his wisdom.

Contents

Foreword

When I first met Ray, and we shared our leadership approach, I felt like I had found my brother. We could start and finish each other's sentences. I've never met another leader who shared such deep moral character and concern for YOU, the reader. Ray and I are in search of the best ideas and inspiration to guide us on our life journeys. You can call our chance meeting serendipity or luck, but after a short period of time, we simply call each other friends. I realized Ray's depth, breadth and deployable approach to leadership is uplifting to all. I continue to learn from his sage wisdom.

Ray's visible intensity and search for excellence were the traits that originally caught my eye, but it was his humanity and willingness to give of himself that touched my heart. A champion is never measured by the number of times they hit the canvas, but whether they have the strength of will to get up and continue the contest. Ray always stands up, and does so with such dignity and grace, that he serves as an inspiration to all around him. I count myself among those blessed individuals who have become better versions of themselves because they have known Ray Zinn.

I fully support, endorse and encourage ALL to read and deploy the essential nuggets of gold found in The Zen of Zinn.

— David K. Williams, Chairman and Chief Executive Officer of Fishbowl

Introduction

wisdom, noun: knowledge of what is true or right coupled with just judgment as to action; sagacity, discernment, or insight; wise sayings or teachings; precepts.

Humans acquire *knowledge* in many different ways, ranging from formal education to learning helpful hints to raw hands-on experience. However, they acquire *wisdom* mainly from other people.

My father was quite good at handing out both. Early in my development he said to me, "It is better to learn by the mistakes other people make than making them yourself." The mathematics behind this is undeniable. The cost of failure may be high, but the cost of not failing in the same spectacular way as someone else might be ruinous. My father had imparted pure wisdom because the knowledge – the mathematical aspect – was implicit in his wording.

Wisdom is not mere knowledge. It is knowledge or intelligence honed with perception. With wisdom, you receive perspective, often earned through experience and delivered in a way that makes the application of the knowledge perfectly sensible. As politician James Dent once noted: "Intelligence is when you spot a flaw in your boss's reasoning. Wisdom is when you refrain from pointing it out."

In the *Zen of Zinn*, I offer you my wisdom. As the longest serving CEO in Silicon Valley, I acquired more than my fair share. But before I founded my company, before I led it for 37 years (36 profitably), before learning to see the world more sharply after going blind, I had acquired a wise philosophical foundation. In it, I understood why people are valuable, why kindness creates and does not destroy, how teams require trust, and how people simply tick. I assert that my success in business might not have occurred had these humanistic perspectives not arrived first.

Forming wisdom requires first acquiring knowledge and experience. Oddly though, we *acquire* wisdom from others in the opposite way. We quite often learn a precept, lesson or parable that illustrates the point, then we walk through life seeing how the lesson works. That is why the *Zen of Zinn* is presented in that order. Those humanistic philosophical elements appear after you have absorbed the wisdom that I can offer.

This book is for everybody, though I have a special place in my heart for the entrepreneur, the businesswoman, and anyone working with teams of their fellow human beings. For them, there are specific quarks of wisdom I want to convey.

For the Entrepreneur: It is wise to know that your journey is a marathon and not a sprint. You soon will see that the entrepreneur's life is one of endurance, and you'll see the joy of the journey.

For Leaders: Leading is a people process. For you, I offer some wisdom concerning why people unite for their causes, and why you must be their servant more than their commander.

For Executives: Managing a business, or a department therein, is like piloting an airplane. It is wise to stay focused on the horizon and let your instruments and stall horns help avoid disaster.

For Students of Life: Life is not for the timid. Neither is working with people. But being social creatures, we humans live our lives with and through others. Knowing the intersections is a talent that I hope to improve within you.

Wisdom and knowledge go hand-in-hand. So should wisdom and virtue, for one leads the other. David Starr Jordan showed his own wisdom in saying: "Wisdom is knowing what to do next; virtue is doing it."

Leadership

Humility is an essential human trait. An entrepreneurial CEO who works directly with all of his employees, and who uses servant leadership, remains humble. By focusing on his people to accomplish the corporate mission, and by making himself their tool for completing their work, he avoids the tar pit of egotism. If your ego grows large, it interferes with every relationship including those with your employees.

Are you a leader? Good leaders can tell if anyone is following by seeing if the tasks are met and on time. When you make sure the team is happy and working well together, they will follow.

"Don't give in, give out." "Giving in" is an expression of "I surrender." Rather than thinking of "giving in," think of "giving out." This turns the tables. When you seek to "give out," you are focusing on what is really important ... others.

The first and great leadership commandment is to love your employees as yourself.

❂   ❂   ❂

Employees view negatively a "leader" whose main goal is to become wealthy. People who strive for wealth are typically selfish and self-centered – they put themselves above others. A "leader" is defined as one who gets things done through people. It follows then that a successful leader is one who focuses on his people. Good employees are the engine of his organization. Great leaders make sure that engine is well taken care of. They know that better people make better employees and instead of worrying about their fortunes, leaders worry more about the fortunes and misfortunes of employees and their families.

❂   ❂   ❂

A friend of mine coined a saying that I love: "Blessed are the flexible for they shall not get bent out of shape." This is similar to an ancient Chinese proverb that claims: "Bamboo survives the storm better than the mighty oak, because bamboo has learned to bend with the wind." Being flexible means you are willing to go with the flow — to not resist change. Flexible people are easy to work with because they are accommodating — they don't have to have things their own way. Be happy and be flexible, for the two are united.

❂   ❂   ❂

Leading is more than being the boss. It means you lead by EXAMPLE. This means not asking your people to do anything that you would not do yourself. Subordinates love it when the boss is willing to roll up his sleeves and get his hands dirty.

Are you your own person? Do you stand up for yourself? If you do, then you have confidence. Being confident in oneself is important if you are going to lead others. No one is going to follow a wishy-washy leader. If you don't feel confident in your ability to lead, then no one else will either. Confident leadership is displayed when you are kind, decisive, humble, knowledgeable, positive, and respectful. Be a good leader. We need good leaders.

Quality is a term that is most often used with a product. I want to focus on quality leadership. Product quality is easier for managers to understand, but quality leadership often gets diluted with more obvious and measurable characteristics, like sustaining revenue growth and profitability. Yes, these are quality leadership characteristics, but they don't tell the whole story. The more admirable characteristics are having honesty, integrity, dignity and respect for every individual, vigilance (doing whatever it takes), and working to boost employee morale. A quality leader is admired by all of those he or she leads. They literally would be willing to give their life for their leader, if necessary. This is because the quality leader is willing to do the same for his or her employees, and often does. Are you, or will you become, a quality leader?

If you consider winning as causing others to lose, then you are a competitor. If you call winning helping others to win, then you are called selfless.

Guiding principles are extremely important, whether it be for an individual, family, company, community, or nation. As the term "guiding principles" suggests, they are precepts that guide individuals or organizations throughout their lives in all circumstances, irrespective of changes in defined goals. In the case of organizations, irrespective of strategies, its type of work or leadership is the guiding principle.

These guiding principles should be held sacrosanct and unchangeable. They should stand the test of time. They define who we are and what we stand for.

At Micrel, a company that I founded and ran for 37 years, we had the following guiding principles:

- Honesty
- Integrity
- Dignity and respect for everyone. (No foul or condescending language was permitted).
- Doing whatever it takes: no excuses.

As you can tell from this list, these principles are everlasting. They apply to each individual and every organization within the company.

Now, what are your guiding principles?

To ask or to tell, that is the question. To ask someone to do something is a request. To tell someone to do something is a demand. They are each taken differently. They both can accomplish the same thing, if there is mutual respect. I prefer to be asked, not told. If someone has to tell me to do something, it is usually because asking hasn't worked. To avoid being told what to do, make sure you understand what is being asked by repeating the question. This does two things. This turns around a demand response to an ask response, such as "take out the trash" to "oh, would you like me to take out the trash, please?" Asking builds consensus, where telling disrupts consensus. To ask is to be kind. To tell is to be condescending.

One leadership challenge is to get people behind something they normally would be reluctant to do. In most cases, this is all about change.

People hate change, and it takes special leadership skills to get people onboard. So how does one get people to accept change?

A great leader embraces change and promotes it enthusiastically. Change will only be accepted if leadership supports it wholeheartedly. His vision and the necessary changes need to be fully explained and justified.

When properly communicated, change can be achieved and supported by everyone.

Some leaders get things done through intimidation, some through means of force, while others use charisma, charm. Charisma is defined as exercising charm that inspires deep devotion in others. Both work, but charisma is preferred by everyone. So how does one develop charisma? Charisma is earned. Those who develop it are usually kind and inspirational. You just love them and want to be around them. You will do almost anything for them. They do not come across as demeaning or intimidating. They garner your support and, quite literally, your devotion. You know who they are; and you know if you want to be like them, you will need to emulate them.

During a recent interview, Cam Newton, the quarterback for the Super Bowl-defeated Carolina Panthers was asked why he was such a poor loser. Cam said, "There is no such a thing as a good loser. A loser is a loser." What the reporter was really asking was, "Why can't you be a gracious loser?" Whether we are winning or losing, we need to be gracious. To be gracious means we are being kind and tactful. I am appalled at the way people can, and too often do, treat one another. This is vividly displayed in the terrible rhetoric circulating in political campaigns. You can help by being gracious toward your fellow man at all times.

Whether we are winning or losing, we need to be gracious.

The great leaders I know have a "steady hand." They don't get flustered. They speak in a calm, deliberate voice. They don't use condescending language when addressing others. They are loved and respected. People just want to be around them.

Some leaders just want to lead. It is all about them. They only seem to care about themselves. They just want to be the boss. This is the opposite of "servant leadership." Real leaders lead by taking care of their people. It is less about themselves and more about those they lead. They are truly humble, caring, and are "willing listeners." They listen more and talk less. Real leaders won't promise you the moon and deliver you a stone. They are cherished and not loathed. They are like a good parent: they teach correct principles and then let the people govern themselves. Be a real leader and have happy followers.

What we need are more "righteous" leaders. A righteous person is one who has good morals, is virtuous, and is of excellent character.

In business, we all too often pick leaders who have credentials to lead but who lack virtue. There is an enormous difference. Righteous leaders are humble, thoughtful, not arrogant; they are kind, respectful of all persons, never vulgar or condescending, and are more about serving than leading.

Isn't this the kind of leader you would like to be, or you would desire to have lead you? If you are in a leadership position, be a righteous leader.

Being alert and attentive is the hallmark of a great leader. Great leaders are aware and concerned for their people. They treat them with dignity and respect. In turn, they are loved and respected. A great leader is truly a servant leader. They lead by example. They are honest and have deep integrity. They are selfless and thoughtful. Being a great leader is to be sought for — over any other accolade that can be bestowed upon us.

☯ ☯ ☯

It rarely matters what you believe or think, because you are not on the same page as other people. People are in different situations at any given point in time. Because of that, we see things differently. Many people, when trying to make a choice, will vacillate before reaching their final decision. They are controlled in part by their mood, perspective, and situation at any given time. We humans are the proverbial vacillators. Trying to catch us all in the same mood, with the same perspective, in the same situation, is next to impossible. But a good leader helps focus people, unite perspectives and thus get everyone on the same page.

☯ ☯ ☯

The expression "seamless transition" means that a transition was executed so well people didn't even know it took place. This expression comes from the clothing manufacturing industry where a seam is formed. If the seam was sewn with great care, then you won't be able to see it. If two businesses or organizations are merged with little or no hiccup, this is deemed a seamless transition. But what good are seamless pants, if the rest of the garment is in tatters? To make a seamless transition, we need to make sure we don't damage the fabric of the organization. Truly caring leaders are sensitive, make the transition seamless and leave the binding fabric intact.

☯ ☯ ☯

What kind of a leader are you? Do you like, love, or feel indifference toward those you lead? They can tell. The single biggest reason people give for being unhappy with their job is their supervisor. If you are an employee who is unhappy with your supervisor, you are not alone. Your only real solution for this is to find other employment. Like a leopard can't change his spots, a poor supervisor has a difficult time changing his or her people skills. If you are a leader, regularly check on your people skills. To do this, the best way is to have someone else outside your department talk with your employees to get their view. Do this often and regularly.

☯   ☯   ☯

All change is internal, be it within a person or an organization. The change agent may come from external stimuli, but without reflection on the causes and effects, the person or the organization will not change. In a company, it is up to the leadership to see, understand and communicate both the stimuli and the desired change, so that all employees obtain the desire for change.

☯   ☯   ☯

Keep the "faith," as the saying goes. Faith is that genuine human characteristic that rallies support from the troops. They love it when the boss expresses "faith" in them. A good leader instills trust, confidence and a "can do" attitude among his people. Lead them, guide them, and walk beside them. They will kill themselves to support you.

☯   ☯   ☯

A plan without a purpose is a waste of time. This happens when we feel the need to keep busy or believe that busy work is good. Every day should be filled with meaningful and purposeful activities. Have a goal to do something good every day. This is best accomplished by planning your week ahead. Then stick to this plan without hesitation. If you do, you will get more out of life and out of others.

Leadership is about getting consensus, not about telling people what to do. We sometimes believe that leaders are benevolent dictators. While this sounds possible, it is not being a leader, much less a servant leader. A servant leader does not need to be a dictator, benevolent or otherwise. A servant leader rolls up his sleeves and works *with* his people. They are, in fact, benevolent. They are respectful to a fault. They encourage and energize their people. People will often follow a servant leader when they don't particularly agree with the task. This is because the servant leader is loved and respected in return.

Teamwork is one of the most important elements in running a successful company. I am reminded of the Budweiser wagon with its beautiful stable of Clydesdale horses. They are a wonder to behold. The wagon master, who I liken to a CEO, is able to drive his team through a complex maze of obstacles with incredible precision. The driver and horses are a masterpiece of teamwork. Like the Budweiser wagon master, a good leader who knows the art of developing teamwork, can lead his people through the very complex maze of business obstacles with the same precision. The art of developing teamwork starts with the business leader loving his team. He or she garners the respect of the team when dignity and respect are shown to each member of the team. No condescending language is ever used. There is loyalty and trust amongst the team. Be a great wagon master, and lead your team to success.

Be a coordinator, not a dictator. Whether you are running a small business or a department, it is collaboration and coordinating leadership techniques, rather than top-down autocracy, that count. When teams are small, they rely on everyone's specialized skills and talents. It's difficult, if not impossible, to run roughshod over them. As their leader, they will respond better to you if you act like a member of the team rather than the boss. You will gain their respect and they will follow you to the bitter end … if you roll up your sleeves and help them.

As a leader, you can underestimate the impact you have on others. When I retired after 37 years at the helm of Micrel, I was deeply touched by the letters employees sent me expressing how I had made a difference in their lives. Former employees talked in particular about how I fostered an environment of respect and how everyone worked to create a sense of family. As a CEO, I believe we have a responsibility to positively impact the lives of our employees. It should be part of our legacy.

You can eat an entire elephant, but you have to do it one bite at a time. When any task seems overwhelming, take a step back and examine it in small steps, rather than looking at is as a monstrous undertaking. It is the giant leap phenomenon that keeps us from progressing. Overcoming these giant barriers begins by breaking down problems into chucks – bite sized pieces – that you can easily handle, and which are not as intimidating. This turns you from being a problem watcher into a problem solver.

You are known by your dominant personality trait. What is yours? Kind, patient, grumpy, negative? You can be a very helpful and loving person, but if your dominant personality trait is negative, it will wipe out all those other wonderful traits you have. Make sure your dominant trait is positive, and it will cover all those less desirable traits you may have.

Mean what you say and say what you mean. Don't double-talk. When communicating with others, our message must be clear and straight-forward. Avoid using flowery, verbose or complex words. Use words that everyone will understand. You want your audience to hear the message and not spend time deciphering your words.

A good and quality leader is loved, not feared. He is kind and fair. He's a willing listener. He sets the example and leads by example. He is loyal to his people and does not use condescending or vulgar language. He is respected for his knowledge and wisdom. He is truly a people person. Take the leadership test. What kind of leader are you?

Want to get more out of your employees? Praise them sincerely and frequently. One of the main reasons employees give for leaving their company is they don't feel appreciated. So, if you want to reduce employee turnover, try praising them frequently and sincerely. People prefer to work where there is an atmosphere of respect and kindness.

"Are you really in favor? Is this really what you want? Are you sure?" We ask these questions because we have doubts regarding the issue. It is not clear to us that this is the right way to proceed. To this I reply, "are you sure", which is a way of saying, "do you know what the real issue is?" But in many cases, we question other people's decisions based on our own limited understanding. When this is the case, we need to ask ourselves if we are giving them the benefit of the doubt. Before jumping to an unwanted conclusion, let's be more thorough in our understanding of the issue.

How do you reinvigorate? Every great leader has his or her habits. Winston Churchill took baths, Einstein and JFK both took naps, and Gandhi meditated every day. Life is increasingly complicated, so take the time to develop habits that keep you focused and help you reinvigorate — in other words, habits that will help you do the Tough Things First.

"Ours is not the reason why; ours is but to do or die." This old military saying, taken from the Tennyson poem, "The Charge of the Light Brigade," says you are not to question your orders but to follow them to the tee. Being obedient is the first law of leadership. You didn't get to become the leader unless you followed orders. Without obedience in your organization, you can't have harmony. Harmony drives discipline. Discipline drives unity, and unity drives consistency. Consistency drives quality and service, and these two are the most important attributes revered by customers.

❦   ❦   ❦

Companies often get so caught up in selling or trying to make their revenue numbers, they forget about marketing. So just what is marketing? A major part of marketing is your brand. Your brand gives you long-term traction. With the advent of ubiquitous social media, you can enhance your brand better than at any time in history. The downside of this is that every other company is also doing this, causing customers to suffer sensory overload. So, to get your fair share of the public's mind, you need to be judicious and persistent in your social media marketing. Don't be impatient or discouraged if your social rankings do not shoot up right away. Just hang in there and it will happen.

❦   ❦   ❦

"Make up your mind!" We have all said this when we are impatiently waiting for a decision. This urgency can lead to the decision-maker making a hasty decision and perhaps a poor one. Usually this impatience comes because we have already made up our minds, and we just want the other person to ratify it. Being impatient is a bane to good communication. It literally shuts down communication. To get the most out of communication, we need to be willing listeners and not willing talkers.

❦   ❦   ❦

Bragging is a form of dishonesty. Bragging is the excessive and boastful talk about one's possessions or accomplishments. So why do we brag? Apparently, we feel the need to elevate ourselves over others. It is generally brought on by low self-esteem. It is habit forming and difficult to break. Just like any other human characteristic, there are different levels of bragging but still, bragging it is. I have heard people say, "Oh, I am not bragging; I am just telling the truth." If you talk about yourself, be careful, others may think you're just bragging. To avoid being a bragger, keep your comments simple and only talk about yourself when others ask about you. Even in this case, be humble in your answers.

They say that no news is good news. This may be true if you have a medical problem and you're waiting to hear back from the doctor. But, if you are waiting to hear back about a job opportunity, no news can be very bad news. Waiting for news, no matter what the issue, can be very agonizing and stressful. If you are the one responsible for providing the news, just imagine how painful you would feel if the shoe were on the other foot—and you had to wait for someone to get around to notifying you. Even if you don't have all the information, an update is always appreciated. In our minds, we all think the worst, so we aren't disappointed. Get back to people immediately and often and reduce their anxiety.

"All aboard" is a saying that comes from the passenger train days. The train was leaving the station and would depart whether passengers were on board or not. This same philosophy can be applied to leader commitment to get company projects on board. Better to not just hang around the station believing the project can't go forward without the leader on board – get on board.

Entrepreneurial Lift

This is the essence of the entrepreneurial spirit: If it looks like an impossible task, with determination, with practice, you can overcome the impossible. You simply must find the discipline to do it.

An entrepreneur has vision for his or her life and business that is not focused on financial gain.

Building a company is more important than building a product. The hardest part about getting a business off the ground is establishing a reliable customer base with revenues. Most startups think that it begins with developing a product. This is foolish logic. Micrel, the company that I founded and ran for 37 years, didn't even have a product in the beginning. We developed our first product seven years later. In that first seven years, we assembled a solid, functioning company. This included developing a reputation, a reliable customer base, and solid revenues with profits from the start. At first, we offered services, skipping Research & Development expenses while laying our foundation. Without that foundation, the products would have had a tougher time finding customers. Build a good company foremost; then develop products.

Organizations need leaders at every level. Even your most process-oriented teams have informal leaders. The question is how your organization identifies and nurtures the new crop. As some employees rise, leave or retire, gaps will occur. Developing leadership skills in managers is a process every organization needs to develop, so no employee is left without a direct and daily source of guidance and inspiration.

The world is full of dreamers and doers. Which are you? Dreamers are hoping something happens, and doers make them happen. It is okay to have a dream. Even Martin Luther King had one, and it was beautiful. However, dreamers are a class of people who just rarely make their dreams come true. Doers, on the other hand, make dreams a reality.

Whenever we start a new job or business, we are excited and pumped up. However, as time goes by, excitement fades into reality as the shine wears off. The challenge is keeping the same excitement that we had when we started. To stay excited, once the honeymoon is over, requires us to focus on making something about the job or the business new and interesting every day. Having run my own company, I made every day exciting by focusing on how I could make a difference. Whether it be a marriage, a job or a business, make it fun and interesting by finding new ways to make a difference every day.

Great companies don't look for the short-term fix or quick profit. They are in it for the long haul.

People can get lost when in unfamiliar territory. This is usually caused by the following reasons: they have no map; they don't keep track of where they are; they have no clear destination in mind; they have no plan. Taking care of these issues is analogous to running a successful company. You need a good plan (map), you must know your market (the territory), and you should have your sight on the objective (vision) for the company. Don't get lost; know your stuff.

Do we learn by failing? This all depends on how we react to the failure.

Since failure generally results from improper execution, we first must understand why we failed to execute properly. If we can't or won't, then it is unlikely we will learn anything from failure. This leads people to say things like "been there, done that" to avoid trying again. Alternately, we will fail once more, if we do try again without first analyzing our past efforts.

We all make mistakes, and it will only be those who learn from their mistakes who will benefit from failure. Great people aren't afraid to make mistakes. They learn from them and don't repeat them. Don't be afraid to fail -- be afraid not to learn from failure.

Breaking the log jam is what good entrepreneurs do well. In business, you are always going to be faced with impediments to your progress. The challenge is understanding where the log jam is and what caused it in the first place. This is where understanding your business pays off. Log jams, unless relieved, can kill your business. Understanding them quickly is key to your success. This is where doing the Tough Things First pays dividends. Most log jams occur because we let little things become big things. By doing those tasks we don't like doing first thing every day, you minimize those log jams that you inevitably face in running your business.

Coming up with the right idea requires setting aside our biases. It is like hitting ctrl-alt-delete on the computer. To make sure we disable our biases, we might have to "soft reboot" ourselves several times. You will know when you have disengaged your biases. It occurs when you can tell if a particular bias is affecting your decision. You will get the feeling that your idea or decision is a good one. You will feel it in your gut.

To build an enduring company, you need an enduring product plan. If you only have a one product strategy, you most likely will not survive more than three-five years.

It takes a multi-product strategy to be a company that lasts. Too many startups put all their eggs in one basket. They create one product, but no follow-ons. Follow-on products must be in the pipeline before you launch your company.

One great idea doesn't a company make.

Have you ever fought what looked like a losing battle? All difficult tasks just seem to be this way. We tell ourselves, "I just can't do this." For this very reason we should not procrastinate doing them. Prioritizing difficult tasks actually becomes easy and fun once we develop the habit. We begin to see tough tasks as challenges. It becomes satisfying to finish them. However, it does take focus and a willingness to do the Tough Things First.

The clouds of doubt hide the sunshine of optimism. Doubt is born out of fear. Fear is born out of ignorance. Yet ignorance is something we can fix. There is no excuse for not being informed. With super easy access to a plethora of information now at our fingertips, we can overcome not being informed. But, we need to be careful that this same easy access to so much information doesn't mislead us with disinformation. There is a lot of disinformation standing between us and the truth. And it is often our biases that keep us from knowing the truth and cause us to believe disinformation. Controlling our bias so we get to the truth requires intense soul searching. Weigh all the facts and seek out the real truth. "And ye shall know the truth and the truth shall set you free."

How bad do you really want it? There is a story about Socrates concerning a student who pestered him, asking how to gain knowledge. Socrates invited the student to meet him at the ocean the following morning. The student arrived early, eager to know the answer to his question. Socrates escorted the student into the ocean, about waist deep. He then pushed the student's head under the water and held him there until the student was violently struggling. Socrates let the kid come up for air and asked him, "What did you want more than anything else while your head was under water?" The student quickly sputtered, "Air!" Socrates then said, "When you want knowledge as much as you wanted air, you'll find a way to get it." The more we struggle for answers, the more likely we will come up with the right ones. Struggling is good! Don't choose an easier path.

The road to success is paved with perseverance!

Perseverance is defined as: "Steadfastness in doing something despite difficulties or delay in achieving success." The key then becomes one of steadfastness. Perseverance is the hallmark of a true entrepreneur. They are unshakable in their determination to make something a success.

When you are steadfast, you are totally resolute, dutifully firm and unwavering. Be a true entrepreneur and pave your effort with perseverance.

Can you work too much? There is a saying that goes: "All work and no play makes Jack a dull boy." Work is good and helps us develop proper ethics. On the other hand, just like a good night's sleep is important for good health, a proper amount of time away from work is also necessary.

There is belief in the high-tech industry that if you aren't working 24/7, you just won't be successful. My wife and I team-taught at a major university recently. During the Q&A, we were asked how I was able to maintain a proper work/life balance. My wife took the question.

She explained that a proper work/life balance is crucial to being successful. She went on to say that I was home at a decent hour and had most meals with the family. In addition, I was always available to help around the house and assist the children with their school work. I didn't work weekends and, as a rule, I was able to do things with the family.

To be truly successful in life, not just at work, we must have the proper work/life balance. To improve my efficiency, I learned to do the Tough Things First. This increased my daily output by 20%.

Have a good work/life balance by learning to do the Tough Things First.

The biggest challenge that all new entrepreneurs face is getting their new business off the ground. This is a daunting task, because of all the unknowns and risks associated with starting a new business. Before starting Micrel, a successful semiconductor company that I founded and ran for 37 years, I started four other ventures. These other four were not very successful for various reasons. The point here is that not every venture you start will be successful. If you want to be an entrepreneur, you have to be willing to accept failure and move on. As the saying goes, "If at first you don't succeed, try, try again."

Overcoming the urge to splurge is important when starting a new venture. Too many founders feel it is important to appear successful even before they are. Thus, their urge to splurge.

The way to ensure you will be successful is to develop the penny-pincher culture. This is a corporate culture where all employees squeeze every penny from every dollar you spend.

Remember, cash is king; and you won't be king very long if you run out of cash.

I love doing difficult things, what some people might consider to be impossible tasks. These tasks are fun because they are challenging. I'm legally blind, but I'm still able to do many things that fully sighted people can't do like writing motivational articles, recoding podcasts, and writing these social media tidbits. Doing difficult or nearly impossible tasks is fulfilling. It keeps your mind active, and you will continue to be a productive individual throughout your life.

Pushing the envelope is a way of saying we can go beyond what we think we can accomplish. This is nothing more than what every entrepreneur does every single day.

In his book, "In Search of Excellence," Tom Peters wrote: "If you're not getting fired, you are just not trying hard enough."

His point was that those who don't push past established conventions don't achieve anything meaningful.

Pushing the envelope involves going from the known to the unknown and a little bit further. You're not going to get rewarded for mediocrity. You get rewarded when you're thinking outside the box.

If you truly want to be successful as an entrepreneur, you will need to keep pushing the envelope every day of your existence.

I was talking with an executive for a major consulting firm today regarding want-to-be entrepreneurs that have a product idea but no go-to-market plan. This is becoming an issue I hear about far too often. If you are thinking about starting a business and have a good product or business idea, make sure that you have a plan that is practical and doable for the next three years. This includes the financing, the customers in hand, and a follow-on product or business strategy that will extend your runway. I would dare say that nine out of ten startups I have looked at over the past 12 months do not have an adequate and sustainable business plan. Be a true entrepreneur and not a want-to-be entrepreneur.

When things look the darkest, and all appears lost, know this: There are many others hoping and praying for your success. You are not alone.

Knowing this means that you have the responsibility not to let them down. So, you must not give up! Likewise, you cannot just sit back and float along, hoping things will get better on their own. You must, with all diligence, do all you can and maybe even more, to overcome the difficulties you face.

Be the master of your own destiny. Take complete control of your life. Go outside your comfort zone. Find ways to serve others, and behold, you will find that your troubles will diminish — and that your life will be more fulfilled and happier.

What is the real reason you are not successful? If this is on your mind, ask yourself: Under what circumstances am I not successful? Usually when we feel this way, it is on one subject — be it marriage, children, our job, a business, a hobby, etc. And, it doesn't happen all at once. Things usually fall apart slowly over time. This is the irony of such events. When things fall apart quickly, we notice it sooner and take action. But, when they come unglued slowly, we don't recognize it until it is almost too late. To this I say: Stay vigilant, and don't wait until things are too bad to fix.

Doubters and backbiters are the bane of humanity. They provide no uplifting or material value. They cast derision on anything creative or new. We can do without them, except they are going to be with us always; so, we have to deal with them. The key, however, is to not let them discourage or dissuade us from our vision, our plan. Tune them out. Don't argue or give them any credibility. Stay the course.

Get it right, and don't be bamboozled by others. Think it through. Does it make sense? We are inundated by the news media and other sources that try to influence our views and opinions. You need to make sure what you are hearing is based on facts and not on opinions made to sound like facts.

How do you know when to pull the plug of a losing venture? There are three ways:

1) You are running out of money and can't raise anymore.

2) It looks like you are not going to make a decent living from the venture.

3) Your gut is telling you, you are done.

If any one of these three ways is what you are facing ... get out!

Do you love what you do? If you don't, you're not going to love what I'm about to say. We spend almost half of our waking hours working. If you don't love what you are doing, you are going to be miserable half the time. You don't have to be miserable. Learn to love the things you hate. In every job or task, there are the fun things and then there are the tough things. To get the most joy out of your job, do the Tough Things First.

Entrepreneurs have laser focus.

I found a quote that I love by Walter Bagehot: "The greatest pleasure in life is doing what people say can't be done." Throughout my life, I have sought doing what others have said can't be done. I believe I am able to do what others won't or can't, because I focus on doing the Tough Things First.

"If you risk nothing, you have risked everything," the adage goes. It is true. If you isolate yourself so you have nothing at stake, you run the risk of never getting anything back in return: no risk, no reward. When investing – in stocks or in yourself – the higher the risk, the greater the return. Be a risk taker and get more out of life.

Understanding cash flow is very important when running a successful company. Most entrepreneurs give too little heed about this, changing their attitude only when they run out of cash. Monitoring cash flow on at least a monthly basis is crucial. It is more than just looking at your bank balance. By analyzing how the cash is used, you will stem the tide of cash drain. First, make up a budget. Then compare the actual monthly expenses against the budget. By looking carefully at each expense category, you will see where the cash is going. Next, be frugal, which is different than being cheap. Most entrepreneurs overestimate revenues. If, at the end of the month, the revenue/income is not as much as expected, per the budget, cut expenses immediately. Prolonging these expense cuts will eat rapidly into your cash, and you will find yourself in deep trouble. The best advice is to stay within your budget at all costs.

"If you follow the flow, you may lose control." This refers to people who decide to let others dictate how they live their lives, by trying to fit into a particular lifestyle or fashion. When you do this, you begin to give up some free agency. It is a slippery slope, so you need to be careful whom you follow. This counts double for venture capitalists.

When visiting a customer, client, friend, partner or relative, try to begin the conversation with a point where you both can agree, like, "It is such a beautiful day, isn't it?" Starting off with a narrative that you both share and agree on is a good way to get off on the right foot. During a conversation, if the discussion gets a bit testy, go right back to a point where you both can agree, such as: "I love it when we can openly discuss things without it getting personal." Then to cement the relationship, end on a positive note, like, "Thanks for the time you spent with me today." If you are always positive and considerate, you will continue to build great relationships.

The expression "That was a learning experience!" is generally associated with a negative outcome or dealing with a significant problem or challenge. It is a way of saying, "I hope I don't get to repeat that again." In my view, all challenges and problems are for our benefit and growth. When I lost my eyesight in 1994, I asked, " Why me?" I really should have said "Why not me?!" While the loss of my eyesight has been a huge challenge, it has helped me grow in so many ways. The next time you are faced with a huge challenge, just say, "Wow, another great opportunity for me to learn and grow."

Have you considered the alternative? An alternative is an option that should be explored, not just lightly considered. Some people call this a fall back plan. I don't. When I started Micrel, it was an alternative to another direction I was headed. My previous venture was a consumer electronics distribution company. It was doing quite well at the time, and I thought it would be a tremendous success. As it turned out, Micrel, a semiconductor company, was very successful while the consumer electronics business, in the end, did not do all that well. In this case, the alternative turned out to be the best. Have an alternative, and you won't get caught holding the bag.

Enthusiasm means to arouse intense interest or enjoyment. Infectious enthusiasm comes from hopeful optimism. It is such a joy to be around optimistic people. Their hopeful optimism is infectious. It causes us to rethink our position and hope for a brighter future. In this world of woe, we need more hopeful optimists. Spread the word of hope. Be an infectious optimist.

As a pilot, the most difficult landings were crosswind landings. They were difficult, because to line up on the centerline of the runaway, you had to cross control with one wing down and lots of opposite rudder to compensate. While crosswind landings are not prevalent, you need a lot of practice to do them correctly, or you could end up dead or seriously injured. In business, we have similar situations to pilots having to practice crosswind landings. The business winds are not always favorable, and we need to practice handling them, so we are ready when our business gets some heavy crosswind. For example, keeping solid cash reserves of at least 15% is practical. Also, regular communication meetings with your employees will help them feel at ease when business gets a little sour. Approach your business each day as if it will have some serious crosswinds. This will prepare you when it does happen. And trust me, it will.

Every day when I get up, I invariably have a number of projects that are difficult. So, what do I do? I "eat the ugliest frog first." I do the toughest task first and get it out of the way. By getting the toughest, hardest, worst, and most difficult tasks done early, this makes the rest of my day fun and interesting. I also improve my efficiency for getting more things done each day. In fact, I see an improvement of 20% more getting done by using this approach. Eat your ugly frogs first and have a great rest of the day.

Don't get in a hurry to succeed. Success comes in small but distinct steps. As the saying goes, "Haste makes waste." Each step in running a successful company is calculated to ensure success. Have a well-defined strategy, raise enough money upfront, have a well-defined culture, love your employees, set the right example, and much, much more.

While hope springs eternal, relying too much on hope and optimism can be disastrous. Sometimes a good dose of pessimism is necessary.

As Andy Grove, Intel's past president says in his book, "Only the Paranoid Survive," you need to have some paranoia or you might ignore impending doom. Take for example, if you have some chest discomfort and you chalk it up to just heartburn, and therefore ignore other possible issues, it could turn out to be a disaster.

While having optimism is a good trait, it can also be a shelter from the truth. Don't be so hopeful and optimistic that you fail to look around to make sure your attitude of hopefulness and optimism doesn't end up killing you.

The employees of a certain company noted that their CEO was going down to the airport during his lunch break every day. Their curiosity was getting the best of them, and they wanted to know why he was doing this. He said simply, "I just enjoy watching things take off under their own power." Having run a company myself for 37 years, I can appreciate this story. As business leaders, we all want employees who are self-starters. Self-starters are those who know what to do, when to do it, and they do it on time. Be a self-starter and get things done under your own power.

As I watch the Olympics, I marvel at the capability of these outstanding athletes. They are literally breathtaking. They are smashing world records right and left. As I reflect on this, I ponder what it is going to take to become a world class entrepreneur in the future. The world is becoming more and more competitive. The new entrepreneur needs to be aware of this, if he or she wants to succeed. You will need to refine and hone your skills like never before. You will need to become world class in your own right, and you will need to start right now. It will take unimaginable determination and vigilance. Are you ready? Then go for it.

I am often asked: What is the biggest regret that I faced as a CEO running a company for 37 years? I find this question interesting because regret is basically an unreconciled mistake. Throughout my tenure as a CEO, I've sought to reconcile all of my mistakes, leaving me with no regrets. If you would like to serve with no regrets, then reconcile all of your mistakes immediately. Do not procrastinate one minute.

I stress the importance of starting the day by focusing on doing the Tough Things First. The tough things are usually the ones we don't want to do, and we therefore procrastinate doing them. By developing a habit of doing the tough things first, this accomplishes two things. First, it gets rid of all those nasty and distasteful tasks that we just dread doing, and second, we learn not to procrastinate. It is a win-win!

So, what's in it for me? I was talking with a friend today about whether or not he should write a book. He said that he's worried about whether or not the book will sell. He doesn't want to go through all that effort for nothing. You never get good at anything, if you don't want to put forth the effort. I am amazed at what Olympic athletes are willing to sacrifice to become the best of the best. Can you just imagine the mindset that it required to be the very best, when there's no guarantee of any financial reward? However, it is sacrifice that brings about extraordinary results. If there is no risk or sacrifice, the opportunity is not worth pursuing. Don't stop trying to improve yourself just because you are unsure of the financial reward.

So, where is your leverage? We all have a special talent that gives us leverage. The problem is that we don't all see it or recognize it. We seem to see it in others, so why not ourselves? Simply because we have our nose too close to the mirror, as they say. To see your leverage, you need to take a step back and look at yourself from different angles. You might ask a friend or family member to help. Finding your leverage is important to maximize your success. So, go find your leverage. You might be surprised at what you learn.

It pays to be happy and have an optimistic attitude. I recently talked to one of my ex-employees. A year ago, he had a full knee replacement. However, he recently got a staph infection and they had to remove the new artificial knee. He has been laid up for over a month in a hospital bed. He will still have to undergo a new knee replacement once the infection is gone. Even with all this, he was jovial and happy. I asked him how he could be so happy and jovial given all that has happened. He simply replied, "How's being unhappy or upset going to help?" This impressed me. He is right! This is a classic of using optimism to fight depression. I say, "Fight on, my friend! You will beat this challenge, because of your optimistic attitude."

"Will you ever learn?" my mother would say. What she meant was: "When are you going to stop doing stupid things?" What is interesting is that we learn through trial and error. The key is that we don't keep making the same mistakes. As Einstein said, "Insanity is making the same mistake over and over and expecting different results." The learning process should not make us afraid to make mistakes, but we should simply not repeat the same ones.

It is the true entrepreneur that explores the edges of the box and is not afraid to try new things for fear of failure.

Are you a boxer? No, I'm not referring to the sports pugilist in the ring. I am referring to the person who can't think outside the box. As you know, a pugilist has to stay within a box or ring. Unless you want to be confined to a ring, you need to get outside of it. To do this, you need to explore the edges of the box and find a way out, if you want to be truly creative. Columbus was told the Earth was flat, until he began to explore the edges of that box. To get outside the box, you need to go from the known to the unknown, and a little bit further. Don't be a "boxer." Be an innovator! Get outside the box.

Do you have a gold standard for your life? Personal gold standards are life principles that are held sacred and ones you live by. These kind of standards or principles help guide you in your daily decisions, such as having honesty, integrity, respect for all people, and doing whatever it takes without excuses. If you have these kind of standards, you will be not only successful, but happy.

Did you get my drift? We say this consciously or unconsciously when we try to get our point across. When you are trying to sell your point, whether it be to get a job or sell an idea, a product or whatever, it is extremely important that your approach matches the needs of the other party. Take the saying: "Try to sell refrigerators to the Eskimos." You need to do your homework. Don't assume you know how to sell a product or idea, or that you can just use the approach that suits you. For example, don't go into an interview in shorts, a tank top and flip-flops just because this is who you are—unless this is the mode of dress for the job you are applying for. Know your audience well, and you will be far more successful.

Some people hate change. They get comfortable with the status quo. In fact, people, by nature, resist change. However, this is the first step toward failure. We can't grow and experience new things if we don't embrace change. True entrepreneurs are change agents. Innovators are those people who go from the known to the unknown and a little bit further. Innovators are like the first men on the moon. Love being the first to do something new. Love challenging conventional wisdom. Be an innovator! Be the first!

Real success comes in steps. It is not like winning the lottery – it doesn't happen overnight. It is a thoughtful and continuous process. It begins with a dream, a vision of what you believe is your destiny. Once you have this firmly planted in your mind, you can begin to develop the plan to get there. It starts with the knowledge you will need. Then you proceed to incorporate that knowledge into a strategy. In other words, what you will need to become that success you have dreamed about. Once you have your plan well thought out, the execution phase begins. And once you begin executing on your plan, you cannot stop or hesitate. You must be persistent, never giving up. You will want to take regular stock of your progress, making the necessary tweaks to your plan.

Can you sleep when the wind blows? A story is told of a farmer who was recruiting a new ranch-hand. One that this farmer was impressed with said that he could sleep when the wind blows. The farmer did not really understand what this meant, but hired him anyway. Not long thereafter, a major storm broke out during the night. It awoke the farmer, who immediately got up and went to get the ranch hand's help. He pounded and pounded on the door to awaken him, but to no avail. The farmer, in disgust, went out himself to gather in the farm animals and the hay. To his surprise, the haystacks were already secured, and all the farm animals were safely in the barn. The next morning, at breakfast, the farmer asked the new ranch hand why he couldn't awaken him, even after pounding on his door? The ranch hand said in a calm voice, "I told you I can sleep when the wind blows." How well are you sleeping?

Understanding the basics in running a business will help you beat the odds. The primary principle in running a successful business is loving what you do. This drives the determination necessary to persist and make your company thrive. Similarly, you must love your employees. Loving your people results in a more dedicated workforce with less turnover.

I have been asked to tell self-deprecating stories about myself while running my company. Is this because people enjoy hearing the stupid mistakes we have made? Or is it that misery loves company? They don't particularly want to hear stories of how we avoided making stupid mistakes. Why is this? Maybe because it is not funny/hilarious to hear how we have avoided blunders. My guess is that those who have made lots of mistakes are more interesting. My advice is not to try being funny. Avoid stupid mistakes at all costs. I promise not to laugh.

Do you feel overwhelmed? Are you ready to throw in the towel? We all feel this way at times. It happens when we take on too much too quickly. Our eyes are bigger than our stomachs. When this happens, it is time to prioritize. This is not as easy as it sounds. Why? Because all those things on our plate are super important, and we shutter at the thought of having to admit we can't do it all. It is like admitting defeat. Well, let's face it. You are not going to get it all done anyway. Prioritizing is the only solution. First, make a list of all those important projects. Assign a priority to all the truly life or death projects and do them first. What you will find is there are very few life or death projects. In fact, I would guess, none. So, at this point, assign priorities to those you can do now and that give you the most feeling of accomplishment. Discard the rest or postpone them to a later date. This is not admitting defeat. It is realizing that we weren't going to get it all done anyway, and the better we feel about ourselves, the more we will get done.

❧   ❧   ❧

We all hate the status quo. Yet we seem to be satisfied with it. Why? I think it is because we embrace the KISS principle (Keep It Simple Stupid). We have gotten so focused on simplifying our lives that we are now embracing the status quo. Where is the challenge in our lives? Where is the adventure? It is challenge and adventure that makes us creative. Creativity spawns innovation. Get out of that comfort zone. Reject the status quo. Be adventurous, be creative. Forget the KISS principle.

Management

Some CEOs, of small and large companies alike, often become high-priced road warriors, busy promoting products, promoting their company and not back home running the show. Unable to escape their desire to be showmen, they delegate the wrong activity – having people not in charge of the mission and vision plan corporate growth, which is all about mission and vision. When I find myself spending more than twenty five percent of the time on the road, I make changes so I can spend at least seventy five percent of the year guiding expansion.

A CEO wants to feel the pulse of the company and be aware of warning signs. He has discipline.

I was asked today how was I able to retain employees so well at Micrel? The simple answer is: I made it a great place to work. Adding to this, we were loyal to our employees and made them feel at home. When you feel at home, you feel comfortable and wanted. Make your company feel like home and you will retain your employees.

"Don't chase the needle," my flight instructor used to tell me. When we hit rough air, the airplane would bounce around and even get a little off course. New pilots often try to make immediate course corrections based on instruments — they chase the needles on their gauges. My instructor calmly grabbed my hand and said, "Slow down. You will make the passengers sick." In life and business, you will encounter "rough air." Stay calm, ride it out, don't make rapid course corrections, and always keep your eyes on the horizon.

How do front-line managers use peer pressure (within their teams) in a positive manner? In other words, what can managers do, so that peers on a team drive conformance while providing help and uplift? This is literally the whole concept of team building. Coaches have to do this with their sports teams. Teams are led, not driven. When you lead, you pull the team with you. When you drive instead, you are behind pushing. Pulling works better than pushing. Pushing is like shoving and rarely works. Leading by rolling up your sleeves encourages others to do the same. Rah-rah cheers also help to get the team hyped.

Is good decision-making an art or a science? In fact, it is both. The "art" part of decision-making comes from practice. It is the ability to "read the tea leaves." This only comes with time and experience. The "science" of decision-making is the gathering of all the pertinent information needed to make a sound decision. It is the antithesis of "flying by the seat of your pants" decision-making. Good decision-makers do not rely on luck. They have made an art and a science out of it.

We all like to be warmed by the sun, especially if we are chilled by the weather. Often in business, things can get rather chilly. It is on these occasions that we need to bring a little warm sun into our company. You can do this by being optimistic and uplifting. Praise your employees even more fervently. Words of encouragement go a long way. Be the warm sunshine in your company, and you will weather almost any storm.

Getting the most out of your brand requires careful attention. What customers respect the most is quality and service. If either of these is not up to par, your brand will suffer. You don't even have to be a company to pay attention to your brand. Whether you are an individual or an enterprise, your brand needs to be protected. So, what is quality and service? Quality is simply the reliability of your product or service. In a word, integrity. Service is how well you treat others, which relies on respect and dignity. Keep these always in mind, because when you don't, your brand will suffer, and it will be very difficult to recover. There is a saying that goes: "For want of a nail, the shoe was lost, and for want of a shoe, the horse was lost." It's the little things that can cause us the to win or lose. Stay on top of your brand.

Are lazy employees good employees? Yes, if you can keep them on task. They take more supervision, but they are also less demanding, tend to be more loyal, and tend to get along better with others because they are less threatening. Am I supporting lazy employees? No, I am just stating my experience. The fact is you are going to have a combination of lazy and ambitious employees. You need to be able to deal with both.

All prescription medication comes with warning labels. But, how many of us read them? Most often we don't, at least not until something happens to us.

This is also true when running your business. For every business, there are warnings that need to be understood and watched for. Here are some of those warning signs:

- Not having three months' worth of operating cash
- Customers are complaining about service and quality
- Employee unrest
- Inventories are too high
- Margins are dropping

These are but a few warning signs that you need to be aware of as you run your business. Don't be one of those that ignore the business warning labels.

Every boss eventually must deliver negative feedback. How it is received depends largely on the relationship the boss and their employee have. If the relationship is based on trust, respect, openness, honesty and a common goal, even negative feedback becomes positive. But it is up to the boss to create this relationship, and to do so long before corrective actions are needed. To not make a human connection, and then you deliver negative feedback, will feel like abuse to the employee.

❧   ❧   ❧

In the higher education field there is a saying: "Publish or die."
The same could be said for companies, though the adage would
be: "Innovate or die."

To have continued revenue growth, companies must breathe
new life into their product offerings. They do this by strategic
innovation. To innovate means to bring changes into something
established, especially by introducing new methods, ideas, or
products. There are several ways to innovate:

- Evolutionary- improving on the existing or established.
  Most companies use this approach. Less risky but slower
  growth.

- Revolutionary- a complete change to existing or
  established. Risky and needs to match company's core
  competence and perceived brand.

- Groundbreaking- a pioneering or new market approach.
  Most risky, but can be very rewarding.

Whichever direction you take, it must be carefully thought out.
Change is ever with us and change we must or be left behind.

❧   ❧   ❧

Most of our long-term decisions are for the future, yet are based
on how we view things today. This is a poor strategy. Our view
of the future through the lens of today can be very distorted. For
example, just because we are healthy today doesn't mean we
will be healthy next year. Yet some people will cancel their
health insurance policy because they feel fine this morning.
Another example is the stock market, which can be a bull this
month and a bear the next. The tough part is that the only
decisions we can make are based on what we know and see

today. To make better long-term decisions, review the potential effects of each choice. Examining all the possible outcomes creates a sharper lens.

There is a natural friction between business bureaucracy and innovation. Bureaucracy exists to keep people from doing bad things. But innovation requires some messiness, and some elbow room. When creating your organization, staging your policies and procedures, and seeding your culture, make sure nothing is so rigid that it causes employees' natural curiosity and experimenter nature to be shunted. Give everyone a chance and the latitude to try, fail and try some more.

There is a natural friction between business bureaucracy and innovation. Bureaucracy exists to keep people from doing bad things. But innovation requires some messiness, and some elbow room. When creating your organization, staging your policies and procedures, and seeding your culture, make sure nothing is so rigid that it causes employees' natural curiosity and experimenter nature to be shunted. Give everyone a chance and the latitude to try, fail and try some more.

When looking for a job, are you looking for money or opportunity? Most employers will soon find out. If your focus is money, your chances are worse in landing the job. Employers are looking for loyalty and thus focus on your job history. If, on average, you changed jobs every three years or less, this will not portray you as a loyal employee. Employers are looking for dedicated team members who have a track record of loyalty. When hiring, be aware of the same desires within each candidate.

The holy grail for any company is to get projects/products out on time. Having run a company for 37 years, it drives me crazy when employees tell me the project/product is running behind schedule. This is a CEO's worst nightmare. But telling employees they have to put in longer hours to catch up doesn't fix the problem, because they are already working long hours.

No amount of cajoling is going to ship product sooner. The effort has to be put in well in advance, even before you start. This is accomplished by better planning. You need to outline all the pitfalls and issues that could come up during the project, so that alternatives can be considered and implemented in a timely fashion.

Invariably, there is one bad egg in every organization, and they can be very disruptive to a team.

To minimize bad egg disruptions, you need to understand what makes them a bad egg in the first place. Some factors are personality related, and others are environmental or job related.

In the case of environmental or job related, these can most often be corrected. Moving the individual into a different environment or job is probably the best approach, if it is feasible to do so.

The bad egg with a personality issue is a much more difficult problem to resolve. If counseling doesn't resolve it, the only option is to kindly invite them to leave.

In any case, bad eggs need to be dealt with quickly or the team and the business will suffer.

How can you tell when someone is listening?

- By their facial expressions. If they are looking like they agree or understand.

- They are taking notes.

- They ask questions for clarification.

- They repeat back what you are saying.

- They are looking directly at you.

- They are not using any electronic devices while you are talking.

If they are not listening, the exact opposite is happening. When you suspect they might not be listening, do the following:

- Ask them a question.

- Stop talking and see how long it will take for them to notice.

- Say something totally off the topic and see if they notice.

- Get up and move around to see if their eyes follow you.

"Things take longer than they really do." This is a saying I have heard over the years. I recently started some construction at my ranch. The goal was to get the bulk of the outside work done before the snows hit. The project was started in August last year. Snow usually hits around the end of October. We figured the project would take three months start to finish. I threw in another couple of months just because things never go right. Thus, we should have completed, worst case, by the end of December. It is now the middle of March, and it still isn't done. As I said, things take longer than they really do, or they will take as long as they really take.

If you're trying to do something intricate, when you can't see what you are doing, this is like literally "operating in the dark." Now imagine you are called upon to do something important, when you don't know all the pertinent facts. Yet, this is the way most problems are resolved ... in the dark! Nobody has 100% of the facts when making important decisions, but the decisions need to be made. While we should proceed cautiously, nevertheless, we must proceed. This takes courage and determination. Don't fall to analysis paralysis. You can do it and do it well!

Finding the right rhythm is important in running a successful company. Employees like to see good balance, consistency, and energy in their firm. This right rhythm is key to having low turnover. Just like in a good orchestra, rhythm is all important to keeping the company tempo. If there is harmony, when you are the maestro, your teams will have rhythm, and everyone works together like a stage filled with virtuosos.

A good boss worries more about what kind of a boss he or she is, rather than how good his or her employees are. The boss looks at the employees as an extension of himself or herself. What boss would curse at his or her limbs, if they weren't doing what he or she wants? Sounds ridiculous, doesn't it? When you look at your employees as extensions of yourself, you are the one in control of these limbs. It is up to you, the boss, to care for these extensions. Make sure you are giving them the right directions. I love my limbs and take good care of them, and you should do the same.

❦   ❦   ❦

Employees quit their job for a variety of reasons. But the number one reason is they don't like their supervisor. The primary reason given is the supervisor isn't fair in the way he or she treats them. For example, the supervisor may talk in a condescending way and not even realize they are doing that. Condescending speech becomes a habit, and this habit is hard to break. This is where smiling, caring and being friendly will really payoff. If you want to keep your employees, show respect for them.

❦   ❦   ❦

The road to success is NOT a straight line. It is filled with twists and turns, ups and downs, hazards, and challenges. Many years ago, there was a treacherous road between Hilo and Kona, Hawaii, they called Saddle Road, which was 60 miles long. The advantage was it saved almost an hour of driving between Hilo and Kona, if you were brave enough. The road was not paved and smooth. It was extremely narrow, filled with potholes and other hazards. It was so dangerous, the rental car companies forbade their customers from using the road. There were very few vehicles traveling Saddle Road, and it was very eerie. If you broke down, there was no one there to help you. Having driven this road many times, I was reminded of the experience I had running my company Micrel for 37 years. It was not for the faint of heart. Running a successful company, much like traveling Saddle Road, takes courage and perseverance. If you want to travel your own Saddle Road to success, be prepared for a long and bumpy ride. If you persevere, the reward is worth the ride. My advice is travel safe.

When you think of the expression, "Can't live with them and can't live without them," what comes to your mind? To me, the word "them" refers to employees, co-workers, and customers. They want what they want, when they want it. It is often a one-way street.

Keeping employees and customers happy and getting along with co-workers is all about relationships. You scratch my back and I'll scratch yours. In any relationship, you need to focus on the other person, rather than yourself. This requires subverting your ego and always being willing to listen and to help. Yet, putting others first is not easy, especially if you are the boss.

It takes extreme humility to let go of your ego and back down to preserve a relationship. But once you master it, your relationships will improve.

The rules of engagement are well known in the military field but are less known in the business arena. Every business needs a set of rules for engagement regarding these areas: dress standards, conduct between groups, conduct with customers, work hours, office cleanliness, personal grooming, standards for company parties, use of personal vehicles for work, and a host of many others. These rules of engagement should be documented and reviewed with all new employees and re-reviewed with everyone annually. This protects all employees, as well as the company.

Over-reaction is never a good thing, but people do it anyway.

In California this past February, we experienced a lot of rain. So much so, we encountered some flooding. But to hear it in the news reports, California was washing away. Sure, we had a few areas with some flood damage, but nothing like the media reported it to be (what some people might call "junk news," which is different from "fake news"). Recently, the East Coast had an unusual cold front come in, called a Nor'easter. They shut down schools, cancelled flights, and again, overreacted to a normal weather event.

Why do we over-react? Because it makes news. We humans love stories and the more exaggerated the story, the more we like it. An old joke says that every good story is exaggerated over time. In the modern news cycle, time has shrunk to minutes. Everything is always reported worse than it really is.

This tendency to exaggerate costs time and money and occurs in most companies. Employees feel a need to overstate their demands, in order to get approval for items they want. This causes the pendulum to swing. When employees exaggerate the need, management understates the need, which can result in the problem getting worse.

As a supervisor, the best way to motivate people is to be their friend. Some managers say you don't want to become friends with your employees. They believe it will inhibit your ability to criticize or reprimand them. This is nonsense. By being their friend, they are less likely to need reprimanding or disciplining. But when they do, you, as their supervisor, will be more empathetic and compassionate in the way you handle the situation. It will then be received more genuinely. Employees who are your friends will work harder, be more loyal, and create less problems for you. Be their friend and have a happier workplace.

There are five things you should ask an applicant applying for a position in your company:

1) Why are you changing jobs? If the applicant responds with a negative reason, this is a red flag. You don't want to hire a negative employee.

2) Why did you pick our company? They should have an in-depth knowledge of your company and the position being sought. If they don't, don't hire them. They didn't come prepared.

3) What are the three top things you look for in a new job? (The right answers are [a] advancement, [b] the quality of the company, [c] ability to contribute. Wrong answers are [a] need a job, [b] more money, [c] a likable boss.

4) Where would you like to see yourself in five years? A good answer is helping the company to grow. Wrong answers are: becoming your boss, making a ton of money, or starting my own company.

5) How did you like your last supervisor? Correct answer is: "I loved him or her." Be concerned about anyone who had a problem with their last supervisor.

Sometimes, conversations are hard to follow. This can be because our mind is not focused on the words or the person.

You might be checking your cell phone or typing away on a tablet. This is very annoying to all parties, causing people to ask, "Hey, are you listening?" It's easy to get everyone engaged. First, put away those cell phones. Ask questions to see if everyone is listening. Look to see if all parties look like they are paying attention. If you are in a listen only mode, don't distract yourself with other work. It's difficult to be a "willing listener" if you are multi-tasking. Communication with others is difficult at best. It takes concentration and a willingness to understand. Be respectful of others and be a "willing listener."

One important attribute of human nature tied to success is called the "responsive nature quotient." People who are very responsive (i.e., get back to you quickly) are by nature very attentive, vigilant and dependable. You can assess the responsiveness of a person by giving them a simple but important task and see how long it takes them to respond. Such simple tasks could include: "send me a copy of your diploma, a picture of your family, a picture of your front yard, your kitchen." Such tasks let you assess their responsiveness as well as other key aspects of their lives.

In every company, venture, or enterprise, there is invariably one or more individuals who are culturally disruptive. They canker the organization by impeding progress and destroying harmony. Whether they are at the top of the organization or the bottom, they need to be dealt with. If they can't be turned around, the entire organization will suffer and will ultimately fail. It only takes one rotten apple to spoil the entire barrel. How should you deal with these difficult people? Short of dismissing them, you can move them aside or invite them to seek professional help. I have rarely seen these tactics truly work, but they are worth trying. Other than that, it is time to invite them to leave.

To sink a boat, it's not the water on the outside that will sink you, but the water that gets inside. We too often blame external forces for our demise, when in fact, it is more likely caused by internal factors: too much debt, costs are too high, wrong market, quality problems, and so on. Before you look at external forces, check inside and see if your boat (company) has any leaks.

There is little difference between marketing and lobbying. In a sense, lobbying is generally associated with influencing politicians. Yet functionally, they are the same. Marketing or lobbying is the effort to influence a party to decide in your favor. Both are forms of pestering and nobody likes to be pestered. To do good marketing or lobbying, you must be aware at what point you begin to pester. This is tricky since a lot of marketing/lobbying is very repetitive, and that's annoying. In social media, one pesky marketing tactic is the use of "modals" that appear annoyingly over top of your computer screen. Really effective marketing/lobbying is when you get your point across, simply and almost unnoticed. Likewise, take care that other actions, ones not intended as marketing or lobbying, do not hurt your brand. All of us, in fact, whether we are professional marketers or lobbyists, are marketing or lobbying ourselves by our daily actions.

To get the most out of your employees, you must do the following every day:

  1) Give them clear directions as to what you expect.

  2) Encourage them with constant reassurance and praise.

  3) Level with them. Be transparent even if it hurts.

  4) Be their friend. Know their families.

  5) Offer to help. Roll up your sleeves.

This kind of employee involvement helped me to have the lowest employee turnover in our industry.

Trials and challenges will beset us our entire life. This is called adversity. Preparing for adversity will minimize the impact that these challenges and trials will have upon us. While I was running Micrel for 37 years, we had five major business cycles. Because we were always prepared for these downturns, the impact was minimal. The company remained profitable during all these major downturns, and I can attribute that to the fact that we were prepared for adversity. If you want to minimize the challenges and difficulties in your life, prepare for adversity versus failing to anticipate it.

Overcoming the urge to curse is a challenge, as anyone who has hammered their thumb can attest. But this bad habit can be curbed, if you focus on the reasons and circumstances that bring about the desire to use profanity. In an office environment, accepting that minor frustrations are not worth alienating coworkers is fundamental; and deciding not to swear is part of the solution.

"You can please some of the people some of the time, but you can't please all of the people all of the time." It is difficult to be a boss that keeps everyone equally happy. However, you can still be admired and well-liked. The primary way is to be viewed as fair, honest, and trustworthy. This is no easy task. When business goes poorly, and it will, you will have to make some tough decisions that will test your mettle regarding fairness. Cutting wages or doing a RIF (reduction in force) is not going to be popular. Here is where your communication skills will be tested. At Micrel, I had to do this a few times over the 37 years I ran the company. It was not pleasant, and I lost sleep over it. Here's what I learned: Make sure that you, the boss, take some of the pain yourself. Cut your salary twice as much as you cut theirs. Most employees would rather take a pay cut than see their fellow employees laid off. Do layoffs as a last resort. Bottom line, be FAIR.

When running a company, remember to be humble. If you don't learn this, you will soon. I learned that people will respect you more, and be more willing to help, when you are truly humble. Humility makes people more caring and forgiving. This makes you more empathic and causes people to want to be around you.

Individuals who whine are difficult to tolerate. They make life very unpleasant. Constant complaining is childlike and annoying. If you can't fix what is bothering them, invite them to leave. To succeed, we need people who are upbeat and optimistic.

We all have imaginary dragons in our life. Like real dragons, they eat away at us. We stew about them, agonize over them, lose sleep because of them. As a CEO of a public company, I faced similar dragons every quarter-end. To fight these dragons, I would ask myself how I felt about my effort. If I felt like I had done my best, I would feel less concerned even if the results weren't that good. "Worry about the things you can control and only be concerned about the rest," is a valuable adage. Not worrying about the things you can't control requires an inner peace that only comes when you are doing your best work.

In business, you need to be bold. "Bold" is defined as the ability to take risks, while staying confident and courageous. "Bold" also means to be straightforward and not wishy-washy. Your employees want a bold leader: one they can admire and follow. To be truly bold, you must be vigilant and never show weakness. This includes being focused and staying on course. Be admired. Be bold.

How important is profitability in running a company? I say that profitability is like air to the lungs. Being unprofitable is akin to

holding your breath underwater. Too many startups believe
they can live off borrowed air. This is like having someone else
breathe for you. If they decide to stop providing air, you will
die. You don't want to depend on others for your air. Be
profitable so you can breathe on your own.

☯   ☯   ☯

Want to hire "good" employees? Then make sure they are
"good" people. So how do we determine who is a "good"
person? They are honest, have integrity, speak kindly about
others, and have a "can do" attitude.

☯   ☯   ☯

How do you hire the best employees?

> 1) Sell them on the job. People want to make a difference,
> and when they believe they can do that in their job, they
> excel.

> 2) Choose appropriately dressed and groomed
> employees, because they care about themselves and will
> show this in their work.

> 3) Ask them how they liked their last job and supervisor.
> Employees that disliked either one, all too often, have
> personality problems. Be wary.

> 4) Ask them what they think is most important to them in
> a new job. A focus on compensation and benefits
> indicates a short-term mentality.

> 5) If they sit forward in their chair, rather than leaning
> back, they have energy and interest.

6) Employees who ask questions, smile, and are polite make the best teammates.

7) Employees who look you in the eye are more likely to be honest.

The best way to motivate your employees and get them to do what you want is to get them to love and respect you. To gain their love and respect, you need to first show your love and respect toward them. This you do by being totally honest and fair with them. Praise them often. Know their families. Smile a lot and be friendly and courteous. Don't have a palatial office or perks. These few helpful hints will gain you more traction with your employees than high salaries or other forms of compensation.

Do you ever wonder if certain people are listening to you? I have found that certain messages we are trying to send are not ones that certain people want to hear. They resist trying to understand what you are saying. They might argue, pretend they don't hear, or just ignore you. This is a common defense mechanism to avoid having to deal with your message. So how can we be more effective when it comes to delivering a difficult message? First, timing is everything. We like to, as they say, "strike while the iron is hot." We are upset and want them to know it. Unfortunately, this is not going to be the best time to deliver a difficult message. Your anger and frustration will be the focus and not your message. To be the most effective, you must have cooled down. You are much more articulate when you have had a chance to think through your message. Second, you need to find a suitable place to deliver the message so that it will not be embarrassing to the receiver. The best practice to get the most out of your message is to deliver it as soon as possible (once you have cooled off). The recipient is more likely to understand your message if they are also in the right setting and frame of mind.

Skimming over a problem doesn't get to the heart of it. People skim more often then they think they do, and often do so unconsciously. When we skim, we more often than not devise a poor solution because we see and treat a surface symptom, not a disease. Conversely, we don't want to over-analyze problems either, as this can result in analysis paralysis and not developing a solution at all, or at least not a timely one. The best way to know if you fully understand the problem is how you feel about the solution. When you feel at peace with the answer, it is likely sound. If you are not at peace, then you know in your gut you missed something.

It's all about the revenue and profit margin, but at whose expense? It is at the employees' expense. We rely on employees to make our customers happy and if the employees aren't happy, neither will be your customers. Employees that are under stress will not last long. Reality then dictates that employees are more important than customers, because without employees you will have few or no customers. Without good, happy employees, your company is doomed.

One key in hiring the best employees is to focus on how well they meet their commitments. Ask each candidate the following question: "Tell me your process to ensure that you meet your schedule/commitments?" If they say they don't give commitments or dates they can't meet, end the interview. The correct answer should be they will do whatever it takes to honor the commitment or schedule. The follow-on question is: "Have you ever missed a commitment or schedule?" If they say yes, ask for the example. If they say they missed the deadline due to someone else's fault, end the interview. We all slip and fail at times – this is only natural. The key is, do we take ownership? To be the best, we all should meet commitments and schedules, and if we don't, we should own up to it and never offer excuses.

Originally, the term bureaucracy came from non-elected government officials running a bureau or department. Since these organizations were considered obstructive and held little purpose, we now associate any organization or group that gets in the way of progress as a bureaucracy. This is why it is important to keep all organizations as flat as possible, to avoid having them becoming obstructive. In addition, make sure the power any organization has is held to a minimum. It is the nature of all organizations to increase their power as a method of self-preservation and their ability to exercise influence.

The Greek word "ethos" is defined as the guiding beliefs or ideals of a community, nation, or society. Every company should have an ethos! A corporate ethos is nothing more than the ethical and moral culture of the company. This ethos may be informal, but it is always better to formally define it so that management establishes the culture as opposed to letting it grow wild. Any good and well-defined ethos must be nurtured to ensure it is properly inculcated into every employee and the daily activities of the company. To ensure your corporate ethos is enduring, you must constantly reinforce these ideals through your personal example. In other words, you have to be totally and completely behind the ethos in word and in deed.

Maintaining a steady hand when running a business is very important. Employees and customers do not like a business that operates in a herky-jerky manner. To maintain a steady hand, one needs to have his/her finger on the pulse of the company. Just like you would want a surgeon with a steady hand holding the scalpel, so should the business leader have a steady hand. It shows control and confidence. Use slow and deliberate moves and you will not "rock the boat."

"The bigger you are, the harder you fall." This quote has reference to bullying. Bullying is one of the worst traits you can have. It happens with "bosses" when they let their position of authority go to their heads. No one likes a bully. They are arrogant, disingenuous, self-absorbed, and above all, unkind and difficult to work for. To avoid being characterized as a bully, even if you don't view yourself as one, get out of your office, walk around and visit with your people. Let them feel your genuine concern for them. If you do this on a regular basis, you will never be viewed as a bully.

"Always choose the right when a choice is placed before you."
This should be the motto of all leaders and executive. Studies
show that the most harm comes to companies from the
dishonest actions of leaders and executives. Being honest is the
very first covenant in the Scout Law. At my company,
"honesty" was the first covenant of our culture. Micrel was
known for its honesty and integrity. You can be smart and
wealthy, but if you are not honest, all of the other great
attributes you may have will get washed away. We all
remember the nickname of Abraham Lincoln. He was known as
Honest Abe. When you have a choice, always be honest.

The Scout Motto is " Be Prepared." Every person, whether an
entrepreneur or a business leader, should live by this motto. As
Silicon Valley's longest serving CEO, I can attest to the value of
being prepared. Micrel survived numerous business setbacks
and downturns because we lived by the precept of being
prepared. While we always hoped for the best, we were always
prepared for the worst. As Andy Grove, one of Intel's renowned
founders and CEO's said, "Only the paranoid survive." Be a
survivor and "be prepared."

Training is more than showing the employee how to do the task
for which they were hired. It includes integrating them into the
culture of the company and helping them understand the
policies and procedures. If you spend time making sure the new
employee is well trained and feels welcome, there is a better
chance that they will be more productive and less likely to

leave. In addition, check up with them frequently to ensure they are still happy and engaged.

I love the expression "flying by the seat of your pants." It comes from the old days when the airplanes lacked sophisticated flight instruments and the pilot had to literally feel the airplane's movements in their backsides. The phrase came to be used commonly for individuals who had to respond on the fly. Or, in a negative way, for persons who didn't have a plan. In either case, have a well- thought-out plan and have a sensitive touch in running your business.

It's good to recognize the power of the pronoun "we." Using "we" in our conversations is so much more inclusive. People feel more involved, less threatened. Avoid using the pronouns "I" and "you" unless the pronoun "we" is not applicable.

My toughest decision is always the one I make at the time. I take decision-making very seriously. If a decision is not important, then why make it? It's called "deciding to decide". Because we face so many important decisions on a regular basis, we shouldn't spend time on decisions that are not material. If we do this, we have freedom to make the most important choices. Looking back over my 37 years running Micrel, I can honestly say that 80% of the decisions that were brought to me could have been made by someone else. If you make all of the decisions for your organization, the important ones are not going to be made well.

I was talking the other day with a fellow who was trying to decide where to take his career. He was struggling with the decision. I asked him if the compensation mattered. He said, "Absolutely." I asked him if it mattered where he lived. He said, "Absolutely." The reason for bringing this up is because we can limit or help the decision process if we set certain parameters. The more parameters we define, the simpler we make the decision process. This is called narrowing down the decision process. Next time you need to make an important decision, get down as many parameters as you can and you will be amazed at how much simpler it will be to make your decision.

One of the least understood customs that we have is called "the best man" at a wedding. It's funny that we have a custom and don't even know why. This one goes all the way back to Medieval times. In those days, the bride's family would try to kidnap the bride away from the groom to determine whether or not the groom's family was strong enough to take care of their daughter. The "best man" was selected to stay next to the bride and groom, because he was willing to give up his life for them. This is the kind of loyalty that we need for employees.

If you want good employees, you must treat them well. Companies believe that good employees are those who do good for the company. This is true, but only if the company is good to them.

"The difficult we do now, the impossible takes a little longer." I love this saying. The cure is to love doing the things you hate. Everything we find tough involves doing the difficult tasks. Most companies and organizations that are not doing well suffer from the malady of not doing the Tough Things First. Once you become accustomed to doing the hard stuff early, you will find doing the impossible becomes easier.

"Go with your gut" is a saying referring to intuition. Intuition is one of the most complex phenomenon of the mind. It really means coming to the right conclusion without guessing. There have been numerous articles written on the subject of "intuition." They are, in fact, all over the place. It goes without saying that the more knowledgeable you are on a particular subject, the better will be your intuition in seeking the right conclusion. Therefore, the better your knowledge, the better your intuition. Knowledge rocks if you have obtained significant wisdom.

Sometimes things aren't as they appear. The other day I went with a friend to pick up his airplane. He noticed an object was hanging down close to the ground near the tail wheel. Thinking it was a radio antenna, he kindly called it to the attention of the airplane mechanic who explained it wasn't an antenna but a static wick that had to be in that location. My friend felt rather foolish until I explained that he did bring the issue up kindly, assuming it could have been a real problem. The only thing he might have done a little better was to ask what the object was rather than jump to a conclusion. A question is often better than a conclusive statement.

Startup Life

Despite covariance in the rate of startup failures with overworked CEOs, the problem persists. Some founders are fanatical when bragging that they work 60–80 hour weeks. Their sense of building "sweat equity" blinds them to the sacrifices they make – to their health, to their marriages, to their families and communities. What they mistake as a successful lifestyle is actually a massive failure.

Be optimistic.

The phrase "go for broke" means to risk everything in one big venture. This is what most new startups do. But with only 20% of startups surviving to maturity, this says that the other 80% gambled investors' money in a flawed business plan. If you are contemplating starting your own company, make sure you have sufficient skin in the game — that you have a financial interest your business's success.

Finding the "sweet spot" in running a business is key to being successful. It takes time, at least three years, to reach this point. Three years is how long – at minimum – one business cycle takes. A cycle is defined as the time it takes a product or service to get developed, introduced, adopted, and reordered. The business "sweet spot" occurs when the results of the product or service meet or exceed the expected results. This will determine if a company will make it or not. It is a statistical fact that nine out of ten companies do not find their sweet spot within the first three years, and thus, are not alive to develop their second product.

"Chasing a rainbow" means going after something that really isn't there. But people do this all the time. They somehow believe that there is a pot of gold waiting at the end. Such wishful thinking leads to a desire becoming so great that people will themselves into believing the fantasy (it works for lottery tickets, too). At this point, panic sets in and they start seeing mirages. I have literally seen people chase their rainbows for years. Don't wait until you believe in fairy godmothers before pulling the plug. In my experience, you should know within a year or two if you are on the right track. Be proactive, question your decision at every step of the way. Don't drink your own Kool Aid.

When all else fails, read the instructions.

How many of you have tried assembling something without first reading the instructions? Sometimes this is successful. But, alas, most of the time, we end up with something that either doesn't look or work right. There is always a sequence that needs to be followed in order for the product to come out right.

This is also true in building a business. Far too often, entrepreneurs attempt to run their new business without first understanding the correct principles that need to be applied, in order to be successful. The correct principles to apply, and the right sequence in which to apply them, are:

- Detailed planning: this creates an enduring company

- Adequate financing: access enough capital to take it to profitability status

- Hiring: find the right employees

- Culture: document a set of standards that will last

- Execution: make sure the business plan is followed

- Review: constantly revisiting the plan to ensure it has legs

Follow these guidelines/instructions to ensure you will have a successful business.

It's all about how you grip the golf club that sends the ball in the right direction. So, too, with running a successful company. Knowing just the right grip makes all the difference in the world. If you grip the company too tightly, you will lose flexibility. You will stifle innovation and creativity and increase employee turnover. Grip the company too loosely, and you will lose control; chaos will set in and failure will ensue. Not too tight or too loose is the strategy. There needs to be a balance.

It takes more than a disruptive idea to be successful. You need a good company behind you. Here is what a good company consists of:

- A well-respected and seasoned professional for a CEO

- A marketing organization that knows your market and customers

- A knowledgeable and experienced finance person

- A good team that works well together, including a person who understands product quality and reliability

Most entrepreneurs fail because they don't have a good company behind them. Having a good product(s) doesn't necessarily mean a good company.

I have had the opportunity to look at many startups, with an eye to invest under my venture group called Tough Things First Ventures. What I have noticed is that most have a product idea but no company behind it. It is a mistake in my mind to want to start a company — without first thinking through the mechanics of building a company and having this in place. Whether you are a sole proprietor or a group of five, you need to think through your company structure. What I mean by this is to have a well-though-out organizational structure and plan for how you intend to go to market. This is called the go-to-market plan: how you are going to sell your product and to whom.

Sometimes, it seems the harder I try, the worse I do. From my experience, this is because the harder we try and don't seem to be making any progress, the more frustrated we get. The more frustrated we get, the more likely we are to make the results even worse. Once you find yourself getting frustrated, it is best to stop what you're doing until the level of frustration subsides. Frustration seldom brings good results.

I was talking with an acquaintance about his six-year-old semiconductor company. They currently have no products and no revenue, so they still consider themselves a startup. Based on my many years of experience, you cannot consider your company a startup after even three years. If you are not on your way to profitability after three years, there is something dramatically wrong with your business strategy. Real companies make money. I know there are some very large so-called companies that have never made money, but yet have huge market valuations. This is a disaster waiting to happen. To keep these kinds of companies afloat requires them to leverage their balance sheets and amass huge debts. Don't be fooled by overvalued, nonprofit companies. They are not infinitely sustainable. The only way to run a real company is make money on a continuous basis.

At GE, Jack Welch had this "fail to succeed amount" he took into consideration when investing in a new project. GE was always doing some pilot or study. He would favor those projects that had a low "fail to succeed" investment.

When I look at a new investment opportunity, I immediately look for the "fail to succeed" amount already spent by the founders. This is usually the amount of money it has taken for the "proof of concept." This pilot or study occurs before the company is officially launched. Unfortunately, too many founders want me to fund the "proof of concept." That is not going to happen. The founders need to risk the "fail to succeed" amount before I jump in.

If you are considering starting your own company, be prepared to do all the groundwork and initial investment first, before hitting up others for money.

❂   ❂   ❂

Running your company "by the book" means having a disciplined approach to leading your company. Learn the ins and outs of successful companies. One of the many tips is the useful accounting tools for doing a regular "cash flow" analysis of your business. A cash flow analysis is sometimes referred to as a funds flow statement. It helps you understand and manage your cash. Running a company without doing regular cash flow analysis is like driving a car on a busy freeway blindfolded. Don't crash; understand cash.

❂   ❂   ❂

Living beyond your means is a common phrase used when talking about families that are struggling financially, when they spend more than they make. This phrase is not only applicable to families but also to companies. Most startups live way beyond their means, and this is why they constantly run out of cash. Just as families should be prudent in the way they manage their finances, so should companies, especially startups.

Remember, Cash is King! You don't go out of business if you
have cash.

The successful outcome of any worthwhile undertaking begins
with preparation. Take any good meal. It may take only a few
minutes to eat but an hour or more to prepare. Spending the
right amount of time in preparing the project is crucial.
Concerns for the manufacturability, cost, saleability, and quality
are absolutely essential. Do the proper preparation, and you
will ensure success. Do it right and don't cut corners.

Go for it! Yes, you can do it! This is your day! We have all heard
these expressions. They mean: Don't hold back. Do it now!
Don't let this opportunity pass you by. Grab that golden ring!
He who hesitates is lost! I have seen so many people, over my
lifetime, that have let great opportunities slip by because of
uncertainty and fear of failure. Often, just doing nothing, is
failure: failure to act. If you go with your gut, you will most
likely do the right thing. This is called intuition. Intuition is the
ability to come to the right decision without lots of information.
None of us knows the future. We must all make decisions based
on the best information we have at the time and of course our
gut instincts.

Starting a company may not be too hard, but keeping it running
is another thing. We all look good at the starting line, but not so
good at the end of a marathon. Starting a marathon can be done
by anybody, but finishing ...very few people can do it.

Most people would not attempt a marathon without working their way up to it. They condition themselves through exercise, diet, and especially training. Training for the race is crucial.

Starting and running a business without proper training is suicide.

I am often asked by startup companies on the best approach to raising money. My recommendation is simply this: do not start your company until you have raised sufficient funds to get the company through proof of concept and achieving profitability within six months to one year. The mistake that most startup companies make is not having sufficient funds and then having to spend an inordinate amount of time raising money thereafter. Startup companies have too few leaders in the beginning anyway, so the distraction of raising money becomes deadly.

Being "meek" doesn't mean you think less *of* yourself, but rather you think less *about* yourself. We spend too much time worrying about what's in it for us, rather than thinking about what's in it for others. I have seen too many entrepreneurs worrying about what they're going to get out of the venture, rather than what others are going to get out of the venture. If we focus more on how others are going to benefit, we will find our ventures more successful in the long run.

Understanding your customer is the key to getting the sale. I have found that the best way to understand the customer is to assume he or she doesn't want to see you. Just remind yourself how you feel when you get approached by a salesperson when you haven't asked, especially those annoying sales phone calls. It is these irritating salespeople that give good salespeople a bad name. To avoid the customer hanging up on you or not be willing to see you, get to know them first: exchange names and pleasantries. Sound helpful and understanding of their time demands. Bottom line, be very courteous.

It is imperative to have both a realistic and detailed budget if you want to run a successful company. You must also be disciplined enough to stay within the budget you designed (a budget is meaningless if you don't.) Your budget should go out at least one year and be reviewed monthly. Inclusive in the budget is the expected income/revenue. If the income/revenue does not exceed that projected in the budget, immediate action is required to cut expenses. Not being this disciplined is one of the biggest – and most common – mistakes new startups make. Too often a founder will convince themselves that income /revenue will improve within the next few months. It seldom happens and suddenly the startup finds itself running out of cash. When this happens, cut expenses immediately by assuming business will not improve in the short run. You can always add back expense when business does improve. But when it does, don't instantly add more expense. Instead, wait until you are very sure business is on the rebound and you have sufficient evidence to support it.

We all have a dominant point of view that influences nearly all of our decisions. It may be our focus on issues of nationality or our take on religious, political, educational, or other topics. But make no mistake about it, our point of view does influence how we think and the decisions we make. It is also very difficult to modify or change our dominant point of view. When we address/market a product, it is important to understand the dominant point of view of the audience we are attempting to address. Bear this in mind the next time you launch your product or idea.

While I was mentoring an MBA student, he asked me how one maps out goals to become a financial success. This is an interesting question since financial success is somewhat arbitrary and highly dependent on the skills and capabilities of everyone. Given this windage, the answer must be generalized. First, focus on being frugal. Save your money like there was going to be a financial disaster coming (there will) and then invest wisely. It will be hard to be a financial success without a decent savings account. Next, you must be able to survive at least two years without a steady income. Even these general goals are no guarantee you will be a financial success. But when you do the Tough Things First, you'll learn about financial success, business success and being a success at life.

Have we fought the good fight? Are we happy with our efforts? Is what we are doing satisfying? These are the questions that we should be asking ourselves every day. This personal introspection is necessary if we are to get the most out of each day.

Can I live without it? Good question. This is what we should ask ourselves before making an important decision. This is a habit that, if properly developed, will not only save us money but time. In my experience, we all tend to be a little too spontaneous: not really thinking through the decision. To be a good decision-maker, we have to overcome the tendency to be spontaneous. Next time you have to decide something, ask yourself, "Can I live without this?" It just might save you a lot of time and money.

We sometimes say, "Let's go back over the plan." We say this when something is not working out as we intended. Rather than continuing a failed plan and racking up regrets, we should regularly review our plan to determine if we are on course — and be willing to alter our plans if we are not.

Do you have all your *business bases* covered? This is a baseball term that teaches that success happens when everything is under control. When running a successful business, you must ensure you have your bases covered. Your business bases include things like understanding your cash flow, employee morale, customer satisfaction, project/product status, macroeconomic effects, market swings, and more. When all bases are covered, you control the flow of the game, strike out your competitors and score big.

What does "proof of concept" really mean? This means that an idea has been scrutinized to the point that it has a high probability of being successful. This testing of our ideas, before we implement them, goes a long way to improving our success ratio. Yet it is not limited to products or businesses – it can be applied to anything. Be more diligent. Do a "proof of concept" on your next idea, be it in management, product development, or improving your personal discipline.

The phrase, "coming out on top" usually refers to succeeding or winning. I believe the phrase comes from a wrestling match where the two opponents struggling – facing each other standing up, then going into the takedown – results in one person ending up on top and usually winning, or at least having the advantage. The person that generally ends up on top is the one who moved quicker into the takedown. So, the lesson to be learned here is: Move quickly or end up on the bottom.

We have all heard the term "barriers to entry." This has to do with the difficulties competitors face getting into a market. Do we have "barriers to entry" in executing our own plans? Some of these barriers are doubt, indecisiveness, laziness and lack of confidence. These become our own worst enemy, an invisible competitor. It is okay to wrestle with ourselves, but not to the point of indecisiveness.

Beware of what you wish for! Most new entrepreneurs are so excited and enthusiastic that they don't understand this very basic and important principle. Hope for the best, but expect the worst. These newbies hope for the best and expect the best. This is not only unrealistic, it means they won't be prepared for disaster when it strikes. Optimism is a driver needed for success, but it needs to be tempered with what all seasoned entrepreneurs know as "street smarts." As we say in business:

"Disaster is always just around the corner." Be "street smart." Be ahead of the curve. Have at least three month's additional cash beyond current expenses, even if you are profitable. If you are not profitable, have enough cash on hand to carry you until you are profitable.

Getting ahead of the game is crucial in running a business. To do this, you need to be able to look ahead: foresee the future to some degree. You will need to understand the micro and macro economics affecting your markets. Understanding business cycles will enhance your ability to get ahead of the game. You have to "know when to hold them and when to fold them," as they say when playing cards.

Most plans fail because we don't plan for failure. Now wipe that frown off your face. You say, "No one plans to fail." Exactly, but we are human and no plan is perfect. When we prepare our plan, we hope for the best but we should plan for the worst. We should have contingencies built into our plans. Remember Murphy's Law? "Everything that can go wrong will go wrong." Plan for failure and you will actually plan for success.

Discipline

It is conventional thinking in Silicon Valley that entrepreneurs need to be passionate. This is an incomplete perspective. The correct thinking is that they need to be highly disciplined and passionate individuals. In life, passion without self-control leads to dangerous behaviors, be it rock climbing without checking your lines or indiscriminately sleeping with many partners. VCs can provide some external discipline, but it is far less complete than a CEO with self-restraint provides; and, it tends to be narrowly focused on meeting investment objectives, not creating lasting enterprises.

People often say that they 'just don't have the discipline' to accomplish things. I say, get over it! Discipline is like any other muscle – you have to exercise it daily in order for it to be effective. So, what are you waiting for? Flex that discipline muscle.

The single most important thing you need to do every day is to do the Tough Things First. Make a short list of things you despise doing today and do them first thing. This will free you up to do all those other things you enjoy doing, and you will end the day on a high note.

Just do it! Don't sit on the sidelines, get involved! We have a limited amount of time here on Earth. Don't waste it. Be known for something, something good that is! There are mountains to climb, deserts to conquer, world hunger to solve. We all have the potential to make a difference in this life. Are you making a difference?

I have heard people claim that others get all the breaks. While there are occasions when luck deals us a good hand, it is not something we should rely upon. Instead, getting ahead in life requires diligence and perseverance. I was asked recently during an interview with eBay radio, "What is the primary key to success?" This may sound like a cliché, but success comes from never giving up. You make your own luck. The way I spell "success" is w-o-r-k.

Doing our best even when we can't sounds like a potential oxymoron, but isn't. Sometimes, circumstances beyond our control prevent us from operating at our best. This could be the result of a physical ailment, family issue or unexpected financial setback. Whatever the reason, these anticipatable problems inhibit our ability to be at the top of our game. In 1994, while on the roadshow to take my company public, I lost my eyesight. I went blind. This was devastating for me personally, as well as for my company. We were at the crossroads of determining whether or not to go ahead with the public offering, given my medical situation. At this point, I could not be at my best. After much soul searching, I decided to go ahead with the IPO. I was bound and determined to do my best, even if I couldn't. Now, looking back over the years since I became legally blind, with this being challenging as it was, I can truly say that I gave it my best even when I couldn't.

Strengthen your weakness by doing the Tough Things First. We all have weaknesses. Some just live with them. I would submit that this doesn't have to be. We can overcome our weaknesses by deciding to strengthen them. This takes effort and a commitment to overcome the desire to procrastinate. Procrastination is just like any other habit. You just have to break it.

Are you longing for a better life? If so, get off your duff and start making it happen. Too many of us waste time daydreaming about a better life, rather than doing something about it. Helen Keller, who was deaf and blind from birth, didn't let her handicap stop her from being a renowned book author. So, wake up and do something more than just daydreaming about it.

We have all heard the expression "The devil made me do it." This phrase gives too much credit to the devil, unless that devil is the one within us. We all fight temporal temptations. When we are tempted to do something we shouldn't, we should think about the consequences — if we are caught, how would we feel? If you seriously try this, you are less likely of doing evil.

◉   ◉   ◉

Many people talk about what we should do every day to improve. They are all good comments, but they lack the focus to help us really do better. I stress how doing the Tough Things First will help us improve our effectiveness. I believe the first two tough things we should do every day is exercise and pray. Exercise strengthens our body and prayer strengthens our spirit.

◉   ◉   ◉

Woody Allen is famous for saying "Eighty percent of success is showing up." This means that every day you are fully present and committed. Make the commitment to fully show up in your work, your relationships, your life.

◉   ◉   ◉

What's stopping you? This is a question I hear being asked all the time. It refers to people who can't seem to make up their mind. Why don't you just go ahead and do it? This is easy for them to say, because it is not their mind they have to make up. Well, they are not, nor can they be, in your shoes. Only you can decide for you. My advice is not to force others to make up their minds with your advice.

◉   ◉   ◉

We do have a choice. We can choose to smile, be courteous, help someone in need, be optimistic, make a commitment, be a positive influence. These are all choices within our control. We need not ask anyone for permission. We can just do it. It is your choice, and you are in control. Make a difference in the world by doing the Tough Things First.

The three most important and yet difficult things to do are:

- Giving a sincere apology when you have wronged someone.

- Never procrastinate even the smallest task. Once you procrastinate even the small tasks, you will inevitably develop the habit to include large important tasks.

- Do the tough tasks first.

I have a saying: "He that repeats the past, fails in the future." Here's why.

Most of us are backward-focused, as opposed to being forward-looking. The basis for this belief stems from the "would have, should have, could have" philosophy. Indeed, hindsight is 20/20 and this can lead to "only if" thinking.

But, we can only accurately predict the future if we have perfect knowledge. I have perfect knowledge that if I put my hand on a red-hot surface, I will get burned. Knowledge and experience enhances our ability to predict the future. This beats guessing every time.

If we don't learn from the past, we are doomed to repeat it. But, dwelling on the past is also problematic. It stymies us. Throttles idle our productivity and prevents us from moving forward.

Learn from the past, but don't spend more time on it than is necessary to learn!

❀ ❀ ❀

Self-control is defined as the control of oneself or one's
behavior, especially in difficult situations. I liken self-control to
a muscle. If not regularly exercised, it will atrophy. Good self-
control, properly exercised, will keep us from harm and
dangerous situations. Things we can do to strengthen our self-
control help us focus on others, rather than ourselves. These
include showing kindness, meekness, humility, gentleness,
charity, and giving service to others. Developing these
characteristics will certainly exercise our self-control muscle.
Develop a habit of exercising self-control and you will live a
happier life.

❀ ❀ ❀

When I was having difficulty in school, my dad would tell me,
"Son, it's time to hunker down." What he really meant was, "It's
time to stop the fun stuff and focus on doing the Tough Things
First." This was hard to do, because I had become addicted to
playing sports. Having to hunker down was not what I wanted
to hear. But because I respected my father, I gave up many
sports and focused on my schooling. This was a wise but
difficult choice that has paid huge dividends. Learning to love
the things I hated gave me the discipline I needed to run my
company, Micrel, successfully for 37 years. If you are not getting
the results you need, try hunkering down.

❀ ❀ ❀

Getting the most out of your job is conditional. Whatever your
responsibility is, know it and know it well. Don't expect the
company to spoon-feed you with lots of information through a
detailed job description. It isn't going to happen. Most jobs are
somewhat open-ended and leave you lots of room for

expanding your responsibility. Trust me; they will let you know when you have exceeded your authority. Until then, just keep pushing the envelope until something starts to give. This is the best way to grow in your position and get that desired promotion. Don't be shy, just keep pushing. Most companies love a doer.

"Keep a stiff upper lip," as the British like to say. This really means: "Don't let your troubles get you down." As a child, when I would whimper and my lower lip would quiver, my grandmother would say, "Ray, keep a stiff upper lip," and I would. When the trials of life are weighing upon you, just straighten up, keep a stiff upper lip and keep moving forward.

We all want to become better people. This is why people set New Year's Resolutions. But becoming a better person doesn't start at the beginning of a new year. It is something you must strive for every day, throughout the year, year after year. Procrastinating your desire to become a better person until January 1st rarely works. If you truly want to become that better person, you will need to fight this tendency to procrastinate.

Can losing ever be more beneficial than winning? The answer is absolutely! When we lose, we vow to become or do better. We learn from our mistakes. The message here is not that we should try to lose to become better, but that we don't give up just because we lost. In the 37 years of running my company, I was beset with losing on a regular basis. I would say that perhaps I was on the losing end of the stick half the time. Given this, I learned and came out so much stronger, each and every time. I can honestly say that I grew stronger through losing, because I didn't give up. Great leaders are tenacious. They are like pit bulls; they never give up. You too can win through losing. Just hang in there!

Studies suggest that it takes just 21 days to form a new habit. What are you waiting for? Start developing a healthy new habit now, and in just three short weeks, you could be that closer to a fitter, healthier you.

All relationships begin with an objective in mind. Whether it is starting a new job, a marriage, school, or anything else, there is an end game. When things go awry, it is usually because the relationship was not clearly defined or understood. None of us are perfect and we need to understand that fact upfront. As the saying goes, "If anything can go wrong, it will." It is helpful to know what can go wrong and define, as much as humanly possible, what those factors are. When we rush into things, that is when we will invariably run into trouble. In any important relationship, it is crucial to analyze all those factors that could go awry, because they invariably will. If you will do this religiously, you will avoid a whole host of problems that tend to come up and bite us.

Don't get distracted by the buzz of the day. We often get off into the weeds when something off interest catches our eye. It doesn't have anything to do with what is important, but it nonetheless causes us to waste valuable time entertaining it. The key is to stay focused on the real priorities and not chase these interesting, yet unproductive, issues.

What is does it mean to hide from the truth? It is an unwillingness to make important changes in your life. We all face the need to make important changes, be it losing weight, exercising more, eating healthier foods, getting more sleep, improving our relationship with others, or a host of other things. Yet for many, it is hard to make these changes. Tackling difficult projects takes discipline and work (a lack of discipline and an unwillingness to work is why many people never get started on important changes). Learning to do the Tough Things First will help you become more disciplined. Once you become more disciplined, you will no longer feel the need to hide from the truth.

Pushing the limits of human endurance is not just running a marathon. It is that day to day struggle to deal with the adversities of life. It is that daunting task of enduring to the end. To get the most out of our life, we all need to learn to love the things we hate.

Where is your line in the sand, the one you will not cross? Such lines are standards of conduct we set for ourselves. But like lines in real sand, they are not indelible. Often these are situational. It all depends on circumstances, so-called situational ethics. We will never lie, cheat, or steal unless it is imperative – a matter of life and death. We tell ourselves to never say never. But, this is where we have the conundrum. Ethics should never be situational, for if they are, they will come back to haunt us. You can't stand on both sides of a fence. Establish your ethics as a line set in concrete; one that will not shift with the whims of the situation.

Being irritated is a sign you just aren't very busy. Busy people just don't have time to be irritated. Think about the times you were very busy. Do you recall being irritated? Irritation is a selfish behavior. You are just not getting things your way. If you can overcome this selfish, nonproductive, self-centered behavior, you will be a happier person, one that others like to be around.

Can rejection strengthen our character? It can if viewed in the right light. Just like resistance helps build muscle, rejection can build moral fiber. That is, if we learn from being rejected. We all have had the experience of going to a car dealership to buy a car. We hate it because car salesmen just can't take "no" for an answer. Automobile sales people make a living out overcoming "rejection." So, what's the secret? They are taught to accept rejection as part of the job. So how does rejection build character? This happens when we learn to accept rejection as a "norm." Don't fear rejection, accept it and move on. If you do, you will build character.

"Should have, would have, could have." This oft-used phrase indicates a lost opportunity, usually in conjunction with a regret. Can we make it through life without regrets? Yes, if we always make perfect decisions. Since we don't always make perfect decisions, we should instead learn by not repeating past mistakes. One good way I have found to minimize repeating mistakes is by keeping a journal. Don't be afraid of writing about your mistakes in your journal. You learn the details of your mistakes by jotting them down, and you can refer back to your notes to reinforce your learning.

Don't get bogged down in the details. This is called getting into the "thin of the thick of things." We usually have enough on our plate without delving into the minutia. This often distracts us from the real mission. We can get so caught up dotting the "i's" and crossing the "t's," that we lose sight of the true objective. You are supposed to stand back and look at the picture, not get so close to it that you focus only on the flaws. Be an objective observer, not a critical observer.

Getting to the bottom of something is the challenge. Sometimes, when we think we fully understand, we have only scratched the surface. I usually assume some degree of personal ignorance before researching a decision. This helps me to not jump to a conclusion. Wrestling with a problem is good. Getting in the habit of looking at the issue from all angles helps you get to the bottom of it all. You will avoid a lot of heartache and disappointment, if you can do this religiously. Get all the facts and make sure they are thoroughly vetted.

Most people think they don't try to feel bad. However, if one steps back and watches their mood as a bystander, then one will see they cannot maintain sorrowful — without actively trying to find justifications for their sorrow. This is not to say denial is a cure for sorrow; on the contrary, we need to be honest about our internal conditions and see them non-judgmentally, to the extent of becoming comfortable with all of our emotions. Ironically, denial gives our emotions power by masking the forces behind our chosen actions. Allow yourself time to acknowledge your emotions, watch them dissipate, make your decisions with the full awareness of your emotions, and they will not be your master.

Where can I find all the answers? We all have more questions than answers. You can't be searching for answers unless you have questions. Questions are good; they stimulate our minds, causing us to ponder. Man's quest for knowledge is never-ending. Having this thirst for knowledge is at the heart of our progression. We can't stand still. We are either progressing or retrogressing. Don't keep your life in neutral; gain knowledge through consistent study throughout your life.

"I am not a bad person. I am actually a very good person." At least this is what people tell themselves, as they struggle with everyday challenges. We all have pluses and minuses as we journey through life. The key is to have more pluses than minuses. To do this effectively, we need to evaluate each project as to how well we did. When we do this religiously, we dramatically improve our performance. This is literally a project-by-project performance analysis to measure our productivity. Professional athletes do this every day at practice. As the saying goes, "You can't expect what you don't inspect."

I was counseling an individual today on a job search. He recently graduated with a master's degree. He has never held a real full-time job yet, and he was extremely fearful of the process of looking for work. In talking with him, it was clear he lacked self-confidence. It occurred to me that self-confidence is an issue that many of us face. I believe self-confidence is tied to our ability to accept change. We get real comfortable with the status quo. We don't like to get out of our comfort zone. Accepting the status quo is just like any other bad habit we need to correct. We need to convince ourselves that being uncomfortable is a good thing. Here again, it is learning to love the things you hate. Break the cycle of the status quo: get uncomfortable.

You have gone too far. You have over-stepped your bounds. You have let your personal goals and desires get in the way of your humanity. This is the sad truth for many leaders and executives. It doesn't happen all at once – it happens a little at a time. But what brings this on? Presumed success. Once you begin to experience some personal success, you begin to feel invincible. You lose humility. It becomes all about you. It becomes an all-consuming craving, and you can't get enough of it. It's like a drug habit. You lose all sense of the humanity that got you there in the first place. If you see this happening to you or to an acquaintance, seek immediate help before it destroys you or them.

A counterirritant is a substitute means of taking the focus off the real problem or pain. I have heard that this is the purpose of biting one's tongue. Of course, biting one's tongue also prevents us from lashing back. Some people resort to alcohol, drugs, and other stimuli to defocus the problem or emotional pain. These types of counterirritants are not good for us. The best way to attack a problem or emotional pain is to face the issue head on and get to the root of the problem. Some problems and emotional pains just take time to resolve. Understanding this, and with the kind help of friends and family, you are going to reach a much better resolution than through artificial counterirritants.

If you can't do the little things right, you won't do the big things right either. One of the first things you should do every morning when you get up is make your bed and do it right. Making our bed first thing every morning will start us on doing the Tough Things First. Such a simple, yet important task gets us off on the right foot. You will be amazed how doing this simple chore, first thing, will help you throughout the rest of the day.

Determination

Passion and wisdom will drive many companies to modest success, but determination creates the strongest of companies. An entrepreneur without determination is an oxymoron, and an entrepreneur who does not invigorate his company with determination will likely never achieve his vision. But like unbridled passion, unfocused determination is a short road to ruin. Being determined, while being unfocused, creates unprofitable work. Determination toward the wrong goal produces the wrong results. An entrepreneur and his organization must have determination, but without wisdom and discipline, the determination will lead both the entrepreneur and his company astray.

Discipline creates the vehicle to achieve. Determination provides the fuel.

Several years ago, a terrible storm caused a research vessel to capsize in the Sea of Cortez. There were eight scientists on board, but only three survived.

They interviewed the survivors, asking how they managed to survive while the others didn't. Their answer is a classic: "We didn't stop swimming."

To survive while others don't is a matter of not giving up.

"Give it more and then some." My dad, would say this to me as I would prepare to enter a competition. He would stress that being prepared is not just getting it done, but going way beyond what I thought was needed to win.

Primarily, it revolved around my running track when I was in high school. I was not particularly physically gifted to run track. However, I had a burning desire to excel in track. It took a lot of practice, training, and determination for me to excel in this sport.

Don't be lulled into believing that all you need to do is "do your best." This is an old cliché that will not make you a winner. To excel in anything requires a willingness to give it all you've got, and then, even more.

There is a sure-fire way to ensure your success. Approach your plan as though your life depends on a successful outcome. In other words, pretend that you have only one shot at making it successful. This view causes you to be more careful and thoughtful about your plan.

In 1994, I lost my eyesight due to a freak medical issue, which left me legally blind. At first, I was angry and filled with despair. I asked God, "Why me?" In time, I learned to understand that while we cannot change the circumstances in our life, we can change how we react to them. There is a saying that goes: "We may not be able to change the direction of the wind, but we can change the sails." Rather than let the circumstances of losing my eyesight become a handicap, I made it into an advantage. As they say, "I made lemonade out of lemons." You may ask, "How do you make lemonade out of blindness?" Due to my lack of vision, because of my eyesight problem, I turned to my internal vision: my ability to love increased; I become kinder and more empathetic toward others. This has increased my leadership skills, and I went on to run a very successful public semiconductor company for an additional 21 years. I learned a very important principle: come what may, and love it. I learned to overcome adversity with a positive attitude.

"Can't" is dead! I love this comment. Whenever there is a task or challenge I face that is particularly difficult, and I want to say, "I can't do this," I just tell myself, "Can't is dead!"

The ability to stick with a task until it sticks with you is the "do or die trying" philosophy. I learned how to do this by doggedly doing the tough things first every day. Doing this and eliminating the "can't" word from my vocabulary.

A television interviewer asked his guests, all successful people, what was their "brand?" One person's answer caught my attention. She was a successful singer and her brand was being a "survivor." Being a survivor captures the essence of all successful people. To succeed, you will have to survive the tumultuous cycles of triumph and failure unflinchingly. Be brave and claim the brand of "survivor."

❂   ❂   ❂

Do you have sheer determination? Sheer in this case means unmitigated. This is what it takes to conquer, to do what others say is nearly impossible. Statistics show that only 10% of new startups succeed. To beat the odds, you need sheer determination. You will need to run on empty, even when your physical gas tank is drained. It will take all the energy and skill you can muster. The common mistake that most entrepreneurs face is misunderstanding that determination matters most.

❂   ❂   ❂

Overcoming the fear of failure is called "confidence." Confidence is born out of courage. Courage is defined as the ability to overcome those things that frighten us. This is why courage gives us confidence. They go hand in hand. To develop confidence and courage is to try different things that are new to you. Get out of your comfort zone. Eat different foods. Take a new route to work. Find new friends. It is all about developing your confidence. Once you boost your confidence, your fear of failure will diminish.

❂   ❂   ❂

What is "fighting the good fight"? Many of life's challenges come to us without our seeking them. They just come to us because of being human and alive. We may not want them, but nonetheless, we must deal with them. This is where the fight comes in. If we battle these life challenges to our last breath, we are "fighting the good fight."

❂   ❂   ❂

Redefining "your best," when your best is not good enough, is all about effort. Usually, when we claim that we're doing our best is when we know in our heart that we are not. It is an excuse for achieving less than an admirable performance. To redefine "our best" requires being honest with ourselves about the effort we are committing. Be honest with yourself and redouble your effort.

❂   ❂   ❂

It's not easy, but I am going to make it! This is what we tell ourselves whenever we are facing a particularly difficult challenge. The saying "Life is no bed of roses" is how we feel at times. The good news is that we all come through it somehow. The key is not to give up, to persevere with a brighter hope that these things too shall pass.

❂   ❂   ❂

It's not fair! People say this when they get punished for something they didn't do. Anytime things go wrong when we don't seem deserving of that result, it seems unfair.

Yet, even though we say it is unfair, it doesn't change the outcome. It is like yelling "ouch" when we hurt ourselves.

Life is unfair because bad things happen to us. Such misfortune is part and parcel to living in mortality. While it is normal to yell "ouch," we need to bear in mind that as soon as the pain subsides, things will go back to normal.

While we may feel that having trials and difficulties is unfair, they are part of life; and in fact, they are for our good, for through them we learn. Go ahead and say "ouch" but keep on truckin.'

"Forever is an accumulation of nows." It is the "now" that builds the future. We can only act in the "now." If we want to build a great future, do the Tough Things First ... now.

John Madden, a well-known NFL football coach said, "Winning is a great deodorant," meaning that winning covers a whole host of screw-ups. Having run a company for 37 years, I can tell you that you can never find out how good or bad you are until you hit rough times. This is when your strengths and weaknesses become vivid. None of us likes to face tough times, but we do need them to show us where we can improve.

Being committed is an unwavering process of sticking to a task until it sticks to you. Giving up is not an option. You stay the course, making slight adjustments along the way. Tenacity is your byword. You are focused and determined. This is how I ran my company for 37 years. We were profitable 36 out of 37 years even through numerous business cycles, the dot com implosion, and one major recession.

Nothing of real value was ever built out of pessimism. As we face each new year, let us resolve to be more optimistic about the future. Optimism is the power to build a lasting future. It gives us the hope we need to work out our differences. We can do it. We need to think the best about each other. We need to look for the good in each other. While there will be differences, they don't need to be obstacles. The power is within us, if we will turn our hearts from anger to love.

"I can't do this anymore! This is just too hard! I am getting discouraged!" These remarks are a sign that you are about to quit. We all get frustrated at times. The urge to quit is perfectly natural, but it must be resisted if what you're doing is a worthy cause. Fighting the urge to quit will be one of the most important struggles of your life. Remember that "When the going gets tough, the tough get going." No one admires a quitter, so get going! You must stick to the task until the task sticks to you.

Are you getting the most out of your time on this earth? This may be the most important question you ask yourself. Are you on the right track? Are you happy with life? These are questions we should ask ourselves on a regular basis – as a way of taking stock. Make it a monthly task. At the start of each month, evaluate yourself and your progress. A proper evaluation will almost always show that certain changes are needed. These changes require focus and your utmost attention. Don't slack off and procrastinate. Do those tasks now! Doing the tough things first is the way to avoid the natural tendency to procrastinate. If you act now, with conviction and enthusiasm, you will become that person you have always wanted to be.

❂   ❂   ❂

I have been often asked how I keep going, when things are going poorly? It is not easy, but the simple answer is: I know things are going to get better, so why give up when things are not going well? If we give up every time things take a turn for the worse, we will never benefit from overcoming adversity. Overcoming adversity is one of the most important principles that we can learn in life.

❂   ❂   ❂

Success is borne out of adversity. I have a saying: "Adversity is like manure; it stinks, but it helps us grow." True success, to be worthwhile, requires a lot of blood, sweat, and tears.

❂   ❂   ❂

Have you ever fought what looked like a losing battle? All difficult tasks just seem to be this way. We tell ourselves, "I just can't do this." For this very reason, we should not procrastinate doing them. Prioritizing difficult tasks actually becomes easy and fun, once we develop the habit. We begin to see tough tasks as challenges. It becomes satisfying to finish them. However, it does take focus and a willingness to do the Tough Things First.

❂   ❂   ❂

Discouragement is the bane of mankind. What causes discouragement is the feeling of hopelessness. We feel like this: "Oh, what's the use?" We are ready to give up and throw in the towel.

The sport of boxing is where the phrase "throw in the towel" comes from. When a boxer's manager or trainer knows the fight is lost, they literally throw a towel into the ring, to signal the referee and the other boxer that they are surrendering. The fight is then stopped by the referee to prevent further injury.

So how does one battle discouragement? You need to have a more eternal perspective. There are always going to be times when it looks like the dark clouds of despair are never going to leave. It is during these times that we must convince ourselves that behind every dark cloud is a beautiful and radiant sun. As the saying goes, "These things too shall pass."

It may take some time to shake the clouds of discouragement, but the more optimistic our view of life is, the faster we can cast away the shadows of despair and discouragement.

I was asked in one of the classes I was teaching this week: How do I continue to keep myself motivated? Because I have been this way almost my entire life, it did cause me to think about the question of "motivation." Motivation is a cause or reason that we act in a particular way. The desire to succeed is at the root of being motivated. I told the class that the intense desire to succeed motivates me to act in a particular way. It is to be persistent and diligent in our activities in the areas in which we want to become the best. When we do this consistently, being motivated to succeed becomes a habit. When you develop the habit of succeeding in your pursuits, you will remain motivated.

Being in the right place at the right time is not all about luck. It takes time and preparation and the willingness to be persistent. The best leaders and entrepreneurs make their own luck in this way. It's all about working it, working it and working it. Persistence and diligence is the mother of luck. It's a real shame when people think that successful people are just plain lucky. There's very little luck associated with being successful. Make your own luck and be willing to put forth the required effort, and you will be successful.

When I was watching the Olympics, I was impressed with the determination of the athletes, especially as I was watching volleyball. They were grim-faced and highly focused. Each player knew his or her role and played so hard, making diving maneuvers to scoop up the ball. I thought to myself, this is the way all businesses should be run: with determination, focus, vigilance, and the willingness to do whatever it takes.

We often think of "strength" as coming in the form of physical strength. But our true and more important strength comes from within. It is the courage and fortitude to overcome seemingly insurmountable obstacles—like the loss of a family member, cancer, or a business setback. The true heroes are those that beat these obstacles and come out on top. Want to be a hero? Take what comes and love it.

One of life's greatest challenges is fighting depression.

Depression usually results from a tragedy. When this happens, we sink into a state of "not wanting to go on." We feel like giving up: throwing in the towel. So how do we deal with depression? Well, at first, it takes a little soul searching. If it is caused by the loss of a loved one, there is period of healing that must take place. We mourn the loss. This is natural. There is no time table for this. We just have to work it out; it is like a sliver that gets under our skin. The quicker we can get that sliver out, the better we will feel.

The best way to fight depression, no matter the tragedy, is to fight the urge to do nothing or give up. Push yourself to stay busy. Occupy your mind with other things. If will you do this, you will be well on your way to fighting depression.

Learning to live with adversity through resilience and peace is an important lesson for all of us. The vicissitudes of life can weigh us down and make us discouraged. Resilience and peace can bring great solace to our souls. I am reminded of the Timex slogan: "Can take a licking and keep on ticking." When you get discouraged thinking all is lost, just count your many blessings and you will smile away those problems.

When we say, "We gave it a lick and a promise," what we are really saying is that we did the job in a half-hearted way. Unfortunately, people are too often satisfied with "a lick and a promise." As my mother would say, "If the job is worth doing, then do it well." Doing things with "a lick and a promise" starts down the path to a very bad habit. Avoid this, and do all of your tasks well, no matter how menial.

Have you ever asked yourself: How did I get here? This happens when we don't have a concrete plan. We get caught off guard, wondering what went wrong. We ask ourselves: Why me? The simple answer is that we don't have our eyes wide open. We are not being vigilant. We are letting things happen to us, rather than making things happen. Keep your life from coming off the rollers by being more vigilant and taking control.

You can't talk your way out of a lie. It requires a very good memory to be a good liar. Even embellishing the truth is a form of lying. Cheating is also lying. I learned as a child: "Cheaters never win." Lying is habit-forming and becomes a lifestyle. You can never be a little dishonest. It will haunt you throughout your life. Be totally honest in all your dealings. It will preserve your valuable reputation.

Upon reflecting on the Olympics, there are some lessons or takeaways for running a successful business. Stay focused at all times. Don't become distracted by unimportant but interesting things. Be a winner by being a good loser. Learn from your mistakes and don't blame others. Look good at all times. How you look is a reflection of your inner beauty and respect. Be humble in winning. Congratulate and praise others for their efforts and accomplishments. Be the best, not just one who tries to do your best.

Life can be like a tragedy at times. It seems like the difficulties we face in life outweigh the joys we experience. The reason for this is that the negative always seems to have a stronger impact on us than the positive. It is like the saying "one rotten apple spoils the barrel." However, to overcome this effect, we need to savor more deeply the joys in life. We need to spend more time counting our blessings. When we do this, we will then overcome the tragedies that will ultimately beset us.

Things take longer than they really do. It is a terrible fact that things don't happen on our time schedules. This is where the saying "Blessed are the flexible, for they shall not get bent out of shape," comes to mind. We all have to deal with schedule slippages. They are a fact of life. So how do we remain flexible? Just take a deep breath and smile. We will soon forget the headache we just had to endure.

When climbing a mountain, they tell you to keep your chin up. This is especially true in life because of the mountains we have to climb in our lifetime. We need to keep our chin up and keep on climbing.

In the bestseller, "When Breath Becomes Air", Dr. Kalanihi is dying of cancer. He says, "I can't go on, I will go on." Many come to this same crossroad where going on is too difficult and we just want to give up, but don't. This is where courage and fortitude help us overcome the natural inclination to "throw in the towel." "Fighting the good fight" is something we must do every day if we want to succeed. You can't go on, you will go on. "It is a do or die" struggle. You can do it.

❂ ❂ ❂

We wait and wait for that call that never comes. Our future
hangs in the balance. We expect something good will happen.
We say, it is our turn. Life can be so cruel at times. Our hopes
and dreams are centered on getting that good news. Too often,
when it does come, the news is not good. So, what do we say?
Better luck next time! We pick ourselves up and move on.

❂ ❂ ❂

I was talking with a friend today about his profession. He
claimed that he was happy doing what he does, but doesn't
believe it is really what he wants to do. This a classic oxymoron.
I am happy but unhappy. He is sticking with his current
profession because he doesn't know what he wants to do
instead. I see a lot of these kinds of paradoxes. We are happy,
and this trumps making a change. The issue, I believe, is the
same as the saying, "Better the devil you know than the devil
you don't know." However, this is like building a bridge to
nowhere. It is unhappiness that brings about change. We need
to get out of our comfort zone if we want to improve.

❂ ❂ ❂

What you did yesterday and what you're going to do tomorrow
are not as important as what you're going to do today. Today *is*
the first day of the rest your life. Get it done.

❂ ❂ ❂

The difference between a goal and plan is that a goal is what we
want to accomplish and a plan is the way we accomplish the
goal. Many of us have goals but no plans to accomplish our
goals. A goal without a plan is just wishful thinking.

I was at a university yesterday where I had a speaking assignment. Afterwards, they had this wonderful musical event. I heard a fantastic solo of the song "Dream the Impossible Dream." Tears came to my eyes as I reflected on its meaning. The song is from the play "The Man from La Mancha." The reason the meaning of the song is so important to me is because when I lost my eyesight, I thought I was done for and that I would never be an effective leader again. I carried on in spite of my lack of vision and the impossible dream became the possible dream. We all face handicaps and difficulties at various times in our lives. But giving up is not an option. We must carry-on and dream the impossible dream; and therefore, we make that dream possible for others.

Being a good citizen will turn national divisiveness around. This involves living the Scout slogan: "Do a good turn daily." There is a wonderful church hymn that I love that begins: "Have I done any good in the world today, have I helped anyone in need?" If we all would try to live according to the Scout slogan, to help before we take, I believe all the divisiveness that we currently endure will abate.

The phrase "face the music" means to have to deal with the unpleasant consequences of one's actions. This is a difficult thing for us to do because none of us like unpleasant things. Many consequences are forced upon us through our own stupidity, like getting cancer from smoking. Other consequences we force upon ourselves through reflection. This is called taking responsibility for our decisions. To accept responsibility is more than just mouthing the words. I am deeply disappointed when someone says they accept responsibility but do nothing about their errors. To accept responsibility means that you will take action that will result in personal consequences on yourself. This is true accountability.

If you are not having a happy life, make it! We all suffer challenges that seem to make life unbearable at times. It is easy to be happy when things are going right. The challenge is to be happy when things look like they are going to heck in a hand basket. So, how do we turn these lemons into lemonade? I know this may sound trite but look on the bright side which is, "These things too shall pass." "Time will heal all wounds." So, be happy even with a turndown face. Just come what may and love it. If you can do this, you will have a happy life, no matter how rough the sledding may be or how high the hill you need to climb.

Government and Society

*Simple and clear principles, the underpinnings of both
corporate culture and company policies and procedures,
rely on the KISS principle: "Keep it short, stupid" (or
"Keep it short and simple" for gentler minds).
Complexity brings its own version of chaos, namely the
chaos of inaction. One only needs to look at the world's
largest bureaucracy – the United States federal
government – to see that when things get overly
complex, they also get stupid. The more complex an
organization makes policy or procedure, the more
opportunity there is for confusion, mistakes, rework or
inaction due to fear of bureaucratic reprisal.
Governments have created such complex mazes of
regulations that most of what constitutes government
"work" involves understanding the regulations and
people asking for more and more clarification.*

How do we unite the divided? Unifying is a huge challenge
when the parties want to stay alienated. In today's world, it is a
case of polarization being whipped into a frenzy of hatred. It is
stoked by the media and hate mongers who profit from the
divisions. If we let these ravenous people win, we all lose in the
end. My advice is to not let rabble-rousers canker your life. Rise
above this fray. Be part of un-dividing the divided.

Tax season! The time of year we all dread. The reason we hate to pay taxes is because we do not believe we are getting our money's worth, that the government is wasting our money. I realize that this is a real aggravation for most of us. Let me try and put a different slant on this. With the exception of some of the money being spent in a wasteful way, most of it, nearly all of it, is spent helping us. These good things are education, protection, roads, bridges, medical research, and many other wonderful things.

We may need to take an antibiotic to help us fight a serious infection. Today we face a chronic infection in our society. This infection can and will destroy us if don't do something proactive to combat it.

This social disease is enmity. Enmity is the feeling of being hostile toward something or someone. This hostility can be in the form of speech or it can be physical. Enmity is borne out of hatred. Hatred can be temporary or long lasting. In either case, it is a real threat to our peace and tranquility.

So, what is the antibiotic we can use to fight this dreadful disease? It is, of course, love. Love is the polar opposite to hate. In my mind, love and hate cannot coexist at the same time. Therefore, if you have love in your heart, you cannot and will not foster hatred.

Take a good dose of the love antibiotic and help fight this national disease of enmity.

Don't do something just because you can. Be careful, especially when you have such power. The use of power comes with great responsibility. Whatever power you wield must be done with dignity and respect for those with whom you have power over. Used in the right way, power can be helpful to others, but it must begin by not lording over others. The misuse of power has proven to be one of the most devastating things that happens to mankind.

Why do some millennials like socialistic programs, such as free education and medical care? For the very simple reason that they have been told over and over again that the older generation has saddled them with a huge national debt and the possibility of little or no Social Security. Of course, their belief is that these free programs, for them, the millennials, will be paid for by higher taxes on the older generation now. They call this payback time. It is unfortunate that these millennials won't accept that they were raised up and provided for by the older generation.

Some years ago, my family went to serve meals at a homeless shelter. My daughter, who at the time was 12, was asked by a young girl if she had a home. My daughter said, "Yes." The little homeless girl said, "Oh, you must be rich." This was an 'aha' moment for my daughter, and for that matter, our whole family. We should consider ourselves extremely blessed, if we do have a home, enough food to eat, clothes, transportation, good friends, and an education. We are indeed "rich" and should be very, very grateful.

Automation will not cause further unemployment in the U.S.
Automation has been with us for more than 200 years, but
workers and the economy adjusted. When the train became
ubiquitous in the mid-1800s, it made obsolete the Pony Express;
but, look at all the other jobs it created. Make no mistake, there
is a transition. But the end result is our lives improve, and
employment ultimately grows as a consequence of automation.
For example, the autonomous car will reduce the millions of gig
economy drivers, but the transformation that autonomous
automobiles will have on daily lives will be short of miraculous.
People who commute great distances won't be wasting time
driving, but rather will attend to other tasks that would not be
possible while behind the wheel.

Sluggish business spending on capital goods is a sign that the
economy is not improving, and that we have entered a long-
term state of stagnation. America is mimicking the same
mistakes that caused Japan's Lost Decade. Until politicians
correct both recent and long-term policy, and focus on the
fundamentals of economic prosperity, the hopes and dreams of
everyone, especially the next generation, will be squashed.

Nobility should not be not defined by birth or some special
circumstance, but by our character. Truly noble people have the
unique and superior qualities of human nature. These qualities
include honesty, integrity, dignity shown to every individual,
and doing whatever it takes — no excuses. This was the proud
culture of my company, Micrel Semiconductor, which I ran for
37 years. As President and CEO, it was my duty to see that this

noble culture was strictly abided by. It was my belief that better people made better employees. At election time, we need to make sure we elect the most noble people to these high positions. We need and deserve only the best.

I have heard it said that "You can't judge a book by its cover." This is what we are doing if we don't dig into the substance of each of our political candidates. I think too many of us say, "Don't confuse me with the facts; my mind is made up already." By listening to only one side of the argument, we cannot judge fairly. It is like sticking our head in a bag and breathing our own air over and over until we suffocate.

Is there such a thing as "righteous" anger? There is, as long as it relates to displeasure with something and not with associated negative attributes, such as hostility. Righteous anger has no venom attached to it. It is not demeaning or full of hatred. It is sometimes referred to as tough love. The angry voices we are hearing during elections are demeaning, filled with hatred and vile characterizations. Do not look at these as examples of leadership or even acceptable behavior.

There appears to be a gap between millennials and the next generation. What's going on here and why? The millennials are often referred to as being narcissistic or having an excessive interest in oneself. This is negative in that it is a selfish, entitlement attitude. They believe that all they have to do is show up at work. Kind of a participation award thing. An example was recently given: the employee was asked to sell five widgets per day, and was instructed that it might require them to make at least 20 calls per day to do that. When asked about the results, the millennial said that they had not sold any widgets, but felt they were successful because they made the 20 phone calls per day. So, the issue is the millennials feel that they are not responsible for the results but should be credited for participating.

We are a nation of selective law enforcement. This is, in effect, a form of "anarchy." Anarchy is a state of disorder due to disregard or non-recognition of authority. Authority in this case is the law. Apparently, political correctness now supersedes the law. When this happens, society breaks down and civil disobedience becomes acceptable. This will divide a nation. I see this happening to us.

I am intrigued by the reluctance of people who are obligated to take an oath. They resist taking oaths for a variety of reasons. For some, it requires placing their hands on a Bible or over their heart. These folks prefer to merely "affirm" that they will comply with the obligations. They somehow believe this is less of a true obligation or legal duty. This is a twisted view. Whether you formally take an oath or affirm you will perform as required, the legal obligation remains. Don't try and weasel out of an obligation by believing your choice of words changes the duty. However you dice it, affirm or swear by oath, you are still under the same obligation to perform as required. Be honest, and it won't matter how you say it.

Winning and losing is about perspective. For example, you can win the battle and lose the war. Sometimes, like in football, we might drop back 10 yards to gain 20. In life, we are always giving up something to get something. In economics, if individual A benefits by the labor of individual B, and as long as individual A's and B's gain are not at a loss, it is considered a good economic principle. An example of this is like going to the barber for a haircut. If the haircut is good and the barber is properly compensated for his time, it is considered a good economic deal. Then this becomes a win-win. Do you think paying taxes is a win-win? It is all about perspective.

Why can't people work together? Is it because they don't want to? These are questions that are raised when there are problems in a marriage, at work, with one's children, within a community, and yes, even with our nation. Holding a selfish position is at the heart of animosity. We believe we are right and "they" are wrong. We don't want compromise. We want a fight to the finish and believe that we will never give in! The problem is, we want the other party to blink first, and they may be as stubborn. Standoffs rarely resolve themselves, and the sooner we realize it, the better off we all are going to be. We need to work together - we must work together - because we are all in this together. So, let's get with the program and work it out!

Divisiveness and the economy are the main issues facing America, and they are both interrelated. A strong economy solves a lot of our social issues. The number one cause of divorce involves financial matters, and we all know how divisive divorces can be. If we can improve our economy, I believe a lot of the animosity we are facing in our society will diminish. Most aspects of immigration are also tied to a weak economy. We can improve most of our social problems once we get the economy moving again, and our candidates should be talking about the economy more than other topics.

There is an old saying that goes, "Practice what you preach." It refers to living by the standards you espouse. But, there is a different twist to this that I would like to address. There are many people who preach one way but live another. For example, many people voted for legalizing marijuana, but would never think of using that drug themselves.

To justify this two-faced view, they use the excuse that they don't want to impose their views on others. It is the "live and let live" mentality. However, this logic has a slippery slope to it. Laws are written to protect us from stupidity and danger, i.e. speed limits and such.

In a society governed by laws, we need to make sure our "live and let live "view doesn't hurt our society or individuals in the society. Isn't it time to "preach what we practice"?

Where is the loyalty? I was asked today at a manufacturing conference, where I was the keynote speaker, "How do companies retain employees, when it appears today's employees don't trust their employers?" My response was, it is a two-way street. Employers must signal to the employees that they are loved and respected. If they will do this, employees will respond in kind. Employees really don't want to change jobs. They only want to be treated kindly and fairly. This builds trust and trust builds loyalty. With this kind of relationship, the U.S. can reduce off-shoring and improve productivity. This is how to make America great again.

I got a ticket for going the wrong way on a one-way street when I was a teen. I was driving in a strange town and failed to notice the one-way signs. Being spunky, I decided to fight the ticket in court. I presented a multi-faceted case to the judge. I explained that I was not familiar with the town, that the sign was very small, that is was dark out. I added that the sign was not located in a good spot, and mentioned that nobody was hurt by my infraction. "So judge, please let me off this one time and I promise not to break that law again." Naturally, this did not work at all. He had my complete driving record in front of him. He gave it a quick scan and said, "You have had a number of tickets this year. I should not only fine you, but I should suspend your license." Faced with the harsh reality of being a teen without wheels, I pleaded to him to just let me pay the fine. What hurt the most was to hear the judge tell me I was a menace to other law-abiding citizens and that I didn't deserve the driving privilege. But the big problem was me. My record had come back to haunt me. I learned at this young age how important it is to always obey the law and excuses would not get me off the hook.

Trust in the world leaders, both in government and business, has fallen to an all-time low. The precipitous decline began in 2008 at the start of the financial crisis. Distrust is a result of people being let down by leaders. These "leaders" are those who have not accepted responsibility for their poor decisions and, in some cases, committed flat-out dishonesty. So what behavior drives mistrust? All too typical, it comes from greed. Greed drives almost every form of dishonesty: lying, cheating, stealing, and every manner of corruption. Until the world leaders demonstrate a willingness to accept true responsibility for their actions, the level of trust will not improve.

Being "interested" means being engaged with intense curiosity. Elections grab all of our interest, but why? It is because we believe the outcome is so impactful to each of us individually. But is this realistic? Not really. Just like the World Series holds our interest for a few weeks, once it is over and the outcome is known, we will soon forget about it. Same will be true after every election. We will all get worked up until this election is over; then we'll moan, groan, or jump up and down for a few days before going back to our lives. Stay interested, but then just relax and get on with living.

"Being put under a magnifying glass" means to come under great scrutiny. However, I think it also means that the things you do are enlarged – they are made bigger than they really are. This particularly applies to business leaders and politicians. Their actions appear exaggerated. Knowing this, business leaders and politicians need to manage expectations very carefully.

Why is it that when it comes to our own individual performance, we are not as demanding of ourselves as we are of others? When flying back to the mainland after a trip to Hawaii, the flight attendant asked us to please take our seats, so we could have an on-time departure. All of us will do whatever it takes to have an on-time departure because we want an on-time arrival; and, we get upset if our departure is late. We expect everyone to jump through hoops to ensure we are not delayed. But a plane full of people still need to be told to take their seats. As a community, we depend on each other to do our part to ensure our mutual success. Do your part. Do it on time, every time.

In any election cycle, you can stay above the fray if you ignore the negative and focus on the positive. Make a list of the important issues and how you would like them dealt with. If you don't know how you would like them handled, then decide which candidate you most trust to deal with the issues, as you would select a bank to hold your money.

"The end of civilities" was how writers of old used to describe the beginning of war. So, where have all our civilities gone? I thought we were on the same team, the human race, but we seem to have quit agreeing to disagree. Instead, we stand ready to fight to the death, or at least it seems that way. When things reach this state, animosity is so great that normality ceases to exist. It is, in effect, a civil war (or an uncivil war, if you will). To turn this around, without the shedding of blood (real or metaphorical), the parties have to back down rhetoric and name-calling. There must be a sincere desire to get along. If not, the animosity will continue to grow until really bad things begin to happen. Let's not go down that dark road.

For evil to prevail, this only requires that good people do nothing. Just as darkness is the absence of light, so too is evil primarily the absence of virtue.

Evil will take over, if we do not respond vigorously and with stronger determination. Just like water falling into creeks, and rivers flowing based on the easiest path of least resistance, evil will find its way when nothing opposes it.

Humans can guide rivulets into a path of our choosing. But it is impossible to change the course of a mighty river. There are streams of evil coursing their way across our dear planet. If we stand by and let them turn into malevolent rivers, they will be impossible to stop.

To keep this from happening, we need to act now or face the consequences.

Valentine's Day is a day we remember those we love. I love this great country that I am privileged to live in. America, you are truly the land of the free and the home of the brave. You have nourished my family for 400 years. You have educated me and my family and have given us so many great opportunities. You are the best and the greatest on Earth. Happy Valentine's Day, America.

People

Truly happy people have found value in their existence. Something – be it love, community, achievement, involvement – has made their time on Earth important, and thus they are important themselves. Most people discover their hearts are at great peace when they are in service to others, be it their children, their aging parents, or even strangers at the local homeless shelter. Employees who dutifully come to the office, work their exact eight hours, mindlessly follow detailed procedures and try only hard enough to meet their MBO scores do not perceive they are valuable. Employees who happily rush to the office where they have the permission to innovate, feel connected to others in the organization, and exceed any MBO expectations ... they know they have value.

There are winners and losers in life. I don't mean wealthy and poor. I am referring to those who make a difference in other peoples' lives. If you are a winner, you will have a positive influence. If you are a loser, you will have a negative influence. Winners should uplift others and help them become better people. Losers are judgmental and selfish. Be a winner by being a willing listener and serving others before yourself.

A child asked his mother if she loved him after she had scolded him. She answered with an emphatic, "Yes!" Confused, he asked, "But how can I tell?" She sat him down and with tears in her eyes said to him, "I feed you when you are hungry. I hold when you are hurt. I care for you when you are ill. I pray for you every night."

The mother then asked the child, "Do you love me?" The child quickly responded, "Oh, yes!" The mother then asked the child, "How can I tell that you love me?" He looked straight into his mother's eyes and said, "I will show you," as he kissed her gently on the cheek.

Is it enough that we say we love someone? Words need to be followed up with convincing action.

Can we really love our enemies? By definition, an enemy is someone who has a hostile opposition or intent regarding us personally. The key word here is "hostile." The intent of an enemy is to cause us great personal harm. Given this is the definition of the enemy, how do we love them? Simply do not reciprocate. This doesn't mean we should not defend ourselves. It means we should not wish them harm. There is so much animosity and hatred in the world that we need to show restraint in our feelings toward our enemies.

There is physical attractiveness and then there is emotional attractiveness. I know people who are not considered physically attractive but are beautiful on the inside or emotionally attractive. They are kind, generous, helpful, humble, confident, cheerful, and optimistic. They are a sheer pleasure to be around. You yearn for their company.

Have you noticed how people respond when you are around? Do they seem happier, more cheerful, more engaged, and energized? Or are they just the opposite? Our attitude has a huge impact on others, and this can grant them confidence they may need. If we are asked to give a motivational talk or counsel someone who is going through a difficult period, we spring into action, put on that bright face and deliver our best confidence-building spiel. This call to action gives us the motivation to build up peoples' confidence. But why wait until called upon? Getting the most out of others should be a daily challenge we take on, and our results are measured in the confidence we lift within them. If you want to be a confidence builder, be uplifting in all your remarks and demeanor as you interact with others. In this way, you will also benefit as you see your own confidence improve.

Who is your favorite hero? It is not necessarily the one you most admire. It could be someone who has had the biggest impact on your life. In my life, my heroes have been my mother and my wife. My mother because of the wonderful training I got in my youth. My wife, because she has been my best friend and greatest supporter. Interestingly, these are both women. This is why I believe women are better than men. All women should be treated with the greatest respect. They are the backbone of humanity. I would not be where I am today without these important women in my life. Thank you to all the wonderful women in this world, who make us hapless men look good.

☯   ☯   ☯

It is all about you! You, are the most important person in your
life. This is because you spend more time with you than with
anyone else. In fact, you spend your entire life with you. Then it
should come as no surprise that you are more concerned about
you than you are with anyone else. This is what can make us
selfish. We are so used to the way we look and act, that it is
hard for us to see our flaws. We hate criticism, or for that
matter, even good advice. When you look at a group photo,
don't you first look at yourself? Others don't really care about
you either because they, in turn, primarily are focusing on
themselves. As Seth Godin said in his blog: "You are neither as
bad or good as you think you are." Are you really only as good
or bad as others think you are? Is your entire persona
determined by others? Think about that. This only reinforces the
necessity for us to improve our interpersonal relationships. To
be truly successful, you need to have great interpersonal skills.

☯   ☯   ☯

There is a significant difference between having a rapport with
someone and just a relationship. The difference is the closeness
and trust. In rapport, there is a much better and closer
relationship. There is a merit of trust when there is rapport.

To garner a rapport with someone, it starts with a good
relationship. To develop rapport is difficult. Here are the steps
to developing a rapport:

- Having a sincere bond

- Developing absolute trust

- Feeling mutual empathy

- Being a willing listener

- Helping without being asked

- Having the other person's back

It is not easy to gain rapport, but it is the surest way to have a lasting relationship.

Don't be ungrateful. People may be praying for what you are complaining about. For example, if you are complaining about issues we face in the U.S., think of the millions who would give everything if they could live here.

If you are complaining about anything, STOP IT! The trials and difficulties we face are for our good and personal development.

Sometimes when we try and help others, it can go south on us. The cynics like to say that "No good deed goes unpunished."

Though I am not a cynic, far from it, this is something I have personally experienced. While such negative returns should not prevent us from helping others, it is a challenge to our motivation nonetheless. I have told myself on numerous occasions to just let it go, because we are all human, even those who receive ungratefully.

Giving is a wonderful thing and we all should continue doing it, but doing so should not come back to haunt us. However, sometimes the best response is to get over it quickly, lest we change and never help anyone again.

"Don't push me!" Have you ever said this? If so, you are not alone. From time to time, we all reach our wits end. If you have heard "don't push me," you need to back off. None of us like to be pushed to a point of anger. Pushing someone that far weakens the relationship. Otherwise, if your intent is to damage a relationship (which you should never do), pushing them to a point of frustration will destroy it quickly. Don't be a pusher if you value the relationship. Instead, be a kind and gentle encourager.

Avoiding getting angry and upset is a never-ending process. Try as we might, it seems to escape us. Why? We all want what we want, when we want it. It stems from our upbringing. If we have become used to getting or having a lot, we continue to expect a lot.

When we don't get it, we get angry and upset and throw a hissy-fit. So, how does one control this emotion to want what we want, when we want it? Not easy! It becomes a bad habit and we know that bad habits are hard to break.

So here are my thoughts on how to break this ugly bad habit:

- Work on putting other people's needs first.

- If you have an urge for something, intentionally postpone the action to acquire it. By doing this, it will help you control this emotion to get what you want, when you want it.

- Be respectful; praise and thank others for the little things they do for you.

Being "offended" is a choice. It is not forced upon us. We have to overtly decide to feel upset, annoyed, or resentful. You can't be offended unless you are angry. Where there is anger, there is enmity. It is becoming "offended" that starts fights. This happens when someone feels they have lost something illegitimately. Something has been taken away from them. They somehow feel cheated. To resist being offended, do as the Bible says: "Turn the other cheek." It is your choice. Others didn't cause you to be offended; you did.

"Son, you are better than that." Being the oldest of 11 children was not easy. I was always expected to set the example. Like most children growing up, I was not perfect. However, my mother wanted me to be perfect. I know what you're thinking: No one can be perfect, because we are mortal. So, as mere mortals, can we be perfect? I say yes, as long as you are willing to repent of your mistakes. By this, I mean be truly sorry, ask for forgiveness, make amends for the mistake and then endeavor not to repeat it; by living this way, you can be perfect.

Do you want to increase your sphere of influence? The sure-fire way of doing this is by not focusing on yourself. Get out of your comfort zone and help others.

"Don't you get it, or are you trying *not* to understand what I am saying?" Understanding what is being said or being conveyed is crucial to good communication. It is only fair to give this your full attention. If you can't because of other pressing issues, kindly ask if you can get back to the other person at a more appropriate time. If you are the one presenting the issue, make sure the receiver is in a place where they can give their complete involvement. Both parties need to be fair and honest when communicating.

Do you consider yourself a happy person? In the workplace, a happy person is admired and sought after. You know if you are considered a happy individual if people enjoy being around you. You smile a lot and you are courteous, kind, and respectful. People seek your advice. So, if you want to be liked, be happy.

One of the great tragedies I have been aware of lately is that people who have a vengeance against someone will pass on false information about them to injure them. No matter what your cause is or your vengeance may be, this does not give you the right to harm another person by using disinformation. You may hate them and not want anything to do with them, but passing on false information is dishonest.

Before you engage in a conversation, you have to be sure everyone is on the same page or the discussion will not be meaningful. Are we debating or discussing? Is there mutual respect? Do we care if the outcome is favorable? What is the purpose of the communication? These are some of the issues to be decided before engaging other people in conversation. And ask yourself, if the conversation is not going to be meaningful, why have it? Honing conversations before they begin will greatly improve your dialogue with others.

How do you go about changing someone's mind? Do you consider where they are coming from? To change a person's mind, they need to want to change. You are "beating a dead horse" if you don't take the time to understand where they are coming from. Don't be in a hurry to persuade them. You might even just give them a hint of the subject before jumping into the meat of it. This will allow them to mull the idea over. Kind of like letting them dip their toe in the water before jumping in. A smiling and tender voice goes a long way to getting over a difficult idea or subject. In most case, always assume the idea or subject needs a lot of tender persuasion. Doing this in all cases will develop the right habit of friendly persuasion.

Can we say "yes" when the answer is really "no"? You can, if you put the conditions under which you will say "yes" like: "Yes, I can pick you up at 2:00," when the request was 1:00. "Yes" is always preferred over "no" when someone makes a request. You appear more congenial and helpful. It takes practice saying "yes" when the real answer is "no."

Why do we think no one is working as hard as we are (is it because we see them goofing off at times but think that we never do)? This is pretty normal. We rarely recognize our own sins.

One of the worst aspects of human nature is greed. It drives other failings. In fact, dishonesty is borne out of greed. Greed is the desire to have something we do not deserve, but want with a passion. Containing the appetite for something we want and don't deserve is called self-control. This is a struggle we all face, but for which we need to develop the skills to win. The best way to develop good self-control is to become kinder and gentler. To see how you stand concerning self-control, ask yourself who is more important—me or other people? If you say others, then you most likely have good self-control.

As a kid, I used to love Superman. I dreamed of having his super powers. He was always there to rescue someone in distress. As I grew into adulthood and started my own company, I learned that we could all be like Superman. Maybe we can't leap tall buildings in a single bound or stop a speeding bullet, but just like Superman, we can rescue others who are in distress. So, what kind of super powers do we have to rescue others? We can offer them comfort and a listening ear, our thoughts and prayers. We can be that superhero to them by being that friend in time of need. Just for today, be a superhero and rescue someone in distress.

Why do people dislike being judged? Because all too often the verdict is wrong. This occurs because we have a bias or lack information. There is a story about man who was on a commuter train with his two young boys. The boys were running up and down the isles, disrupting the peace of the other passengers. The passengers were getting highly agitated and wondering why the father was not controlling his two rambunctious kids. What the passengers didn't know was the young father had just come from the hospital where he learned his wife had passed away. Obviously, if the passengers had all the facts, they might have been more understanding. None of us have all the facts, so we need to be more judicious about being judgmental. Remember that as we judge others, so may we be judged. Give everyone the benefit of the doubt and help make this world a less judgmental place.

As hard as I try not to make mistakes, they still occur even when I am sensitive to the possibility. For example, when I send emails, I read and re-read them before I hit the send button. Even with this diligence, I still create errors from time to time. The reason for this is that I wrote the text, and when I re-read it, my mind passes over obvious errors. This also applies when you communicate verbally. Occasionally, someone will take what I said the wrong way because of how I said it. This causes me to ask myself, "Did I really say that?" I check to discover if I have been misinterpreted or if I said it wrong. It is good policy to assume you may have made a mistake, rather than assume others did. This can be tough because our egos get in the way. Just remember, whether you are communicating in writing or verbally, it is your responsibility to make your message clear.

It is hard, in fact nearly impossible, for people to admit they were completely at fault for a wrongdoing. This is because most people believe that others either aided or abetted them in the wrongdoing. No one likes to believe they are so wrong that they would have committed the wrongdoing without some valid reason or assistance from others. This goes to the human nature of protecting oneself at all cost. They might even say, "The devil made me do it." However, when we hear of others doing the same thing, we are alarmed and disgusted. What issues we see in others, we don't see in ourselves, or for that matter, our kids. Frankly, we have an issue of being totally honest with ourselves. Honesty has to start with us before we can expect honesty from others.

How bright is your personal light? Like the lighthouse that guides ships safely to the harbor, we all have a personal light that guides others. They follow our light, especially young individuals. We need to make sure our "light" is guiding those that follow us, leading them to a safe harbor.

How big is the gap between your actions and your words? Do you walk the talk? Your actions speak louder than your words. Narrowing the gap will speak volumes regarding your credibility. One adage claims that "words without deeds is like a field full of weeds." Make sure your deeds are up to speed with your words and success will follow you.

What's your philosophy? We all have belief systems that drive our actions. They are anchored in how we were raised. The influence might be our religious training, political leanings, family upbringing, our friends, our community, country of origin, and other cultural biases. Nevertheless, this is who we are! This is how we are wired! It affects, in a major way, what we decide and how we act. Understanding other people's backgrounds can help us understand how they have come to their decisions or the way they act. The time we take understanding how other people think helps us to be less judgmental.

The power of saying "please" is so effective. "Please" can get so much more done. It means "Would you be so kind?" It puts the sugarcoating on any request. The request, however, must be sincere and not using "please" in a derogatory or denigrating way; like, "would you please shut up?" Let it be "pleasing" to all by using the word "please" with all our requests.

We all have connections that can help others. For example, I heard from a couple of universities that want to upgrade their cleanroom facilities. Because of my connections in the industry, I was able to put them in touch with a semiconductor company that is willing to donate some equipment. This is a win-win. The students win, and the semiconductor industry wins because of the training the students get. You can make a difference, too. Just share your connections to help others.

Are you a truly tolerant person? Before you answer, let's look at the definition of "tolerance." Tolerance means to tolerate something you may dislike. This includes the ability to not argue, take issue with, or sneer at an opinion or belief with which you disagree. So, are you sure you are truly tolerant? Were you tolerant during the last election? If we are honest with ourselves, we likely conclude we are probably not. However, this is understandable because it is hard to be tolerant. It takes discipline to be tolerant when you feel the opposite. Part of the problem is that it's painful to believe that we are not really tolerant. But that admission is a required step before the real work begins. As a country, as a nation, and as individuals, let's focus on becoming truly tolerant.

There is nothing worth obtaining or achieving that justifies compromising our integrity. Our integrity defines who we are. Once you compromise your integrity, it is almost impossible to get it back.

When I was a young salesman, I had a very important contract pending for my company which was worth hundreds of thousands of dollars. I was told by the purchasing manager in charge of approving the contract, that he would award the contract to my company if I would provide free diaper service for his newborn child for one year. While the amount of money the diaper service cost was very small, relative to total value of the contract, providing that service meant I would be involved in a bribe. I declined his offer, and he promptly dismissed me and awarded the contract to my competitor.

Recently, I read that a very prominent and well-respected government official had to resign because it was discovered he hired expensive chartered aircraft on the taxpayers' dime for questionable uses. While this may not have been the worst thing government officials have done, it nonetheless was a violation of the spirit of his fiduciary responsibilities.

Your good name is NEVER worth tarnishing, no matter what the gain might be.

We have all heard the saying: 'Tis better to give than to receive. But just as important as giving is receiving. The more gratefully we receive help from others, the more likely we are to give back in return – a grateful receiver is also a grateful giver. In societies where entitlements have become pervasive, many people have lost the spirit of gratefulness. During the holidays, gift giving is blessed and kind. But, let's focus on being more grateful for the gifts that we get all year long.

Can "yes" ever mean "no"? It can, if we hang a contingency onto the request. For example, "Yes, I can pick you up at 7:00 but not 6:00." We constantly have to juggle our schedules to help others. We generally want to please people and meet their requests. This will require sacrifice on our part. Be an emphatic "yes" person. You will then see what goes around comes around.

Whining and complaining are at the top of my list of the worst of human attributes. Whiners and complainers are all about themselves — their needs and concerns. They tend to be pessimists and drag others down. I dread interacting with them — they suck up all the room's oxygen. If you have the urge to whine or complain, don't; and instead, make everybody happy.

Why is compromising so difficult? The short answer is because we want what we want, and what we want is generally absolute. This goes to our selfish nature. We dig in our heels because we know what's best even if it isn't. We just can't admit that there are two sides to every coin. We believe in the saying, "if you give an inch, they take a mile." So then, how can compromise be achieved? Simply by showing love and respect for the other person's point of view. This also can be done by reminding ourselves there are no absolutes, except when it comes to physical laws.

Does arguing ever get us anywhere? Sometimes, if arguing is part of the occupation or for safety or preservation. Arguing for the sake of arguing is never good. It inevitably leads to hard feelings. So, how can we effectively avoid arguments? First, ask yourself if the argument is necessary; and then, will you care if it leads to hard feelings and maybe the destruction of a valued relationship? As stated above, arguing is never good and should be avoided.

The one sad aspect to winning is that someone else might have to lose. However, the real goal is to have a win-win outcome. This requires having a gracious and kind attitude. Even in a very competitive situation, there can be a win-win if each side works for it. The focus, in these cases, has to be more about enjoying the competition and less about who will be the victor. If you find that winning becomes the primary focus, you will discover that someone is not going to enjoy the event because it is now a win-lose situation. Find more enjoyment by making your relationships fun for everyone: win-win is always better.

One of the most vile habits that we can have is the use of profanity and vulgarity in our speech. It is not only offensive to nearly everyone, but it also minimizes communication. People tend to turn off speech that is wrapped in bad language. Once they stop listening, communication is also stopped. Eliminate profanity and vulgarity and you will improve your communication.

Do we need to be caught to confess we did something wrong? It would appear that most of us would say yes. I believe that if we felt differently, in other words, if we would confess that we did something wrong regardless if we were caught, this would actually reduce our need to confess. This may, on the surface, sound counterintuitive, but I believe it would reduce our propensity to do wrong things.

We get so caught up with our own importance that we fail to see that others don't quite agree. In fact, the more important we feel we are, the less important we become to others. As in the story *Snow White*, the wicked queen would stare into the mirror and ask, "Mirror, mirror on the wall, who's the fairest of them all?" Hopefully, you are not staring at yourself in the mirror and asking, "Who is the greatest?"

Sometimes, conversations are hard to follow. This can be because our mind is not focused on the words or the person. You might be checking your cell phone or typing away on a tablet. This is very annoying to all parties, causing people to ask, "Hey, are you listening?" It's easy to get everyone engaged. First, put away those cell phones. Ask questions to see if everyone is listening. Look to see if all parties look like they are paying attention. If you are in a listen only mode, don't distract yourself with other work – it is difficult to be a "willing listener" if you are multitasking. Communication with others is difficult at best. It takes concentration and willingness to understand. Be respectful of others and be a "willing listener."

Rejection can be a terrible thing. How we handle rejection is the key as to whether it destroys us or gives us more resolve. Rejection is part of life. We all have to deal with it. It hurts and can cause us not to accept challenges. Some people are so averse to rejection that they will do anything to avoid it. The best medicine I have seen to deal with rejection is to tell myself that it's not me that they are rejecting, it is the message I am delivering. I then examine the way I am delivering the message and find ways of improving the delivery. In many cases, you will get rejected no matter how you deliver the message. In those cases, you just move on. As the saying goes, "You can please some of the people some of the time, but not all of the people all of the time."

Debate is good but arguing is not. When we debate, there is generally no animosity. Issues are aired in a constructive way. However, when we get into an argument, tempers can flair and communication all but ceases. Not arguing requires both sides to be understanding and respectful of each other. This is a challenge because of the desire of each side to win. To keep the discussion in a win-win mode, try to find common ground if the debate starts to get heated. This is called compromise.

I need your help, or do I? People generally overstate their need for help in order to ensure they get the help they want. You can readily determine the real need by ensuring that they are as deeply involved as you will be. It is like the saying, "I won't give you a fish, but I will show you how to fish." This way, the needy have a stake in the game. Yes, they will get your help, but they have to be engaged also.

Most people resist change because they are uninformed. So, the key to accepting change is to be informed. I saw this a lot while running my company, Micrel. The employees who rejected change were the least informed. It takes effort to become informed. If you want to be more willing to change, become more informed.

                ◐   ◐   ◐

Some say the truth hurts, but it shouldn't. The only time that I've seen where truth hurt was when we weren't being honest with ourselves. We need to know the truth, we should seek for the truth, and we should accept nothing but the truth. Looking at in this light will change how we view knowing the truth. As the saying goes, "And ye shall know the truth, and the truth shall set you free." In this instance, knowing the truth frees you from ignorance, whether it be of your own making or the lack of such knowledge. Being truly honest, you should always seek for the truth whether it hurts or not.

Before you engage in a meaningful conversation, make sure all are on the same page. Are we debating or discussing? Is there mutual respect? Do we care if the outcome is favorable? What is the purpose of the communication? These are some of the issues to be decided before engaging in a meaningful conversation. Of course, if the conversation is not meaningful, why are we having this conversation? Honing your conversation skills will greatly improve your dialogue with others.

A "skeptic" is a person who is inclined to question or doubt accepted opinions. We see them all the time in the places where we work. They could be customers, bosses, investors, board members, spouses, you name it. They do not uplift or support us. They are saying, "We just don't believe you." This is especially difficult if we believe we are trustworthy. To gain these skeptics' trust takes a long time and a strong relationship. Not everyone is going to give you the benefit of the doubt. My suggestion is that you assume everyone is a skeptic and treat them accordingly. Skeptics take a lot of handholding and nurturing. You will be surprised how much better you will be at dealing with people if you treat them all as skeptics.

"Crying over spilt milk" is a saying my grandmother would utter whenever I got upset over something I couldn't change. It's like letting out an expletive when we smash our finger with a hammer. It's always easier for someone to say this to us when it isn't happening to them. So why do we do this? Is it because we are so glad it isn't happening to us? It is natural for us to get upset. We hate it when someone tells us to calm down. Why can't they let us get it out of our system? Next time you get the urge to tell someone to calm down, just bite your tongue and let them be. Then, the next time you feel like letting off a little steam, you won't have to feel so guilty.

True joy and happiness comes from being honest in all our dealings, being faithful to our companions, having a healthy lifestyle, being engaged in the community, and helping others. If you think about these, they are nothing more than being truly grateful for our many blessings. Recommit to being forever grateful and show your gratitude by serving others.

Why can't we get along? We all want to happily coexist, but we think this starts with someone else changing. We talk about the need for compromise, then don't. Often this is because compromising certain principles or values is not easily done. But this doesn't mean we have to be mean and spiteful when we are unwilling to compromise on certain issues. There will always be times when we just do not agree. These are the moments we need to try even harder to be civil toward each other. Shake hands, give a hug, and express appreciation for all the good things where we do agree.

Winter time is a good time to reflect on what's most important to us. We tend to slow down in the winter and spend more time inside. This is a good opportunity to build strong family relationships. A stronger family strengthens the community. It helps us endure the challenges we will face. I have a friend who just found out he has Stage IV lung cancer. He told me that it is his strong family and friends that are helping him deal with this new challenge. I am convinced that it's these relationships that help us endure all of our serious moments in life.

☯   ☯   ☯

So, what is the biggest room we have in our house? As a kid, when I was getting out of line, my mother would say, "Ray, you need to go clean your room." I knew what this meant. It meant to stop complaining. For those of you who don't know the answer as to our biggest room, it is our room for improvement. None of us are perfect and have lots of "room" to improve. As my mother would say, "Only perfect people have the right to complain." If you complain, I hope you are perfect.

☯   ☯   ☯

I recently toured the battleship USS Missouri, called the Mighty Mo, which is moored at Pearl Harbor, Hawaii. The tour guide commented on the fact that the nearly 900-foot-long battleship was quite narrow, relative to its length, and asked us why we thought that was. We gave all kinds of reasons, but the real answer was quite interesting. The width of the ship was restricted by the width of the Panama Canal. Here is an example of how things around us can cause us to comply, even though the situation is not personally optimal. This is why being flexible pays. If we want certain things, we may have to rearrange our optimal-ness in order to get things done. "Blessed are the flexible, for they shall not get bent out of shape." Being flexible gives us power to do things we otherwise couldn't do.

☯   ☯   ☯

Have you ever said in frustration to someone, "I have had it! I am done dealing with this!?" There is no doubt that all of us face these frustrating moments from time to time. So, what's behind this? We are angry and fed up. We are venting our frustrations, obviously hoping someone will get the message. Do we just chalk this up to being human? Why can't we deal with our frustrations in a more diplomatic way – say by counting to 10? We can do this and for the good of all. It goes back to not being selfish. Escalating an issue by outwardly showing our anger will not make things better, only worse. Just for today, control yourself by just biting your tongue, smiling and walking away if necessary. Anger and disaster come together in the same package.

What are we arguing about? If it is about a belief that we have, it is no longer an argument. A belief is an opinion. An opinion is nothing more than an unsubstantiated fact. If the unsubstantiated fact or opinion is not readily provable, then stop arguing. It is a waste of time. Beliefs are generally deep rooted and unshakeable. No amount of arguing will ever result in a positive outcome. Arguments, even if not about beliefs, are a huge waste of time. They primarily result in hard feelings and we can do without hard feelings. Rather, find ways to buoy people up and shelve the arguments.

A promise is a promise and must be kept at all cost. Don't get in the habit of "trying" to keep a promise; make it golden by keeping it. When we only "try" to keep a promise, we are, in fact, hedging. You want to be known as a person who always keeps a promise. If you find that the promise date may slip, let everyone know early so other arrangements can be made. Make all of your promises sacred. Just meet them!

☯   ☯   ☯

How long can you hold a grudge? Don't wait too long because grudges canker your soul and keep you from progressing. You will hold a grudge forever, unless you can exorcise it from your mind. This isn't easy, but it can be done. Start by forgiving the person that gave you the reason for the grudge to begin with. "To err is human, to forgive is divine." Be the bigger person ... forgive the grudge maker.

☯   ☯   ☯

Did you or someone you know drop the ball? This usually happens when we are not paying close attention. It might even be a case of taking our eye off the ball. If this begins to happen frequently, it is usually due to becoming distracted by issues in our life that become all-consuming. It might be a serious illness, a problem in the family, issues with finances, or a work-related problem. Whatever the issue, it keeps us off balance. Until the issue(s) gets resolved, we need to be patient and understanding.

☯   ☯   ☯

Making fun of people whether you're teasing or not is unacceptable. Most teasing or bashing comes from a lack of respect for the other person. Perversely, such teasing is geared to make us feel good at the expense of others. We primarily tease or bash when we are angry or upset. This is divisive. It is never good or even acceptable to intentionally hurt another, no matter how much we believe they deserve it. If we want to be considered kind and gentle, we must rid ourselves of the terrible tendency to be mean-spirited to others.

Hiding the truth comes in various forms. It is always dishonest, no matter how genuine the motive. In what ways do we hide the truth? The obvious one is by telling a lie. Under oath we are told to tell the "whole" truth. In other words, not leaving out anything pertinent to the subject. How about not giving it your best? This is a form of hiding the truth. You are in effect disguising your ability. Don't hide the truth.

What does it mean to be "authentic"? Some say it means to be the "real you." I say it means to be the real deal. The real deal means to me that you are "tops," the best there is. I am looking for "authentic" leaders. Those who know how to "walk the talk." The real deal. The winners, not just those that pretend. They are impeccably honest and trustworthy. Whether you are a business or political leader, be authentic, the real deal.

"I love you the way you are" my wife tells me all the time. Does that mean I have no room for improvement? No! What she is saying is, "I love who you are." Are we kind, loving, humble, and helpful? This is what people love. Yes, we all have room for improvement. But to be truly loved, we must exhibit those characteristics that all people love: honesty, integrity, dignity and respect for other people, and then be willing to do whatever it takes.

Smart people are not smart alecks. Sometimes we can be irritating to others if we try to show how intelligent we are. Just because you are smart, you don't have to flaunt it. Smart people are humble. They are considerate. The smart people I know have two ears and one mouth for a reason. You don't learn much when you are talking. Be smart; listen more and talk less.

"I can count on him when the chips are down." The adage was coined by gamblers for when they had bet all their money and needed more, and a friend would supply them with more poker chips. What the adage means is that when you have very few options left, it is important to have people that you can depend on. Cherish these people and be one yourself. Be there for someone when their chips are down!

Sometimes, to change our lives, we need to change ourselves. When we get stuck or in a rut, we often blame others or our situation, while in fact, the problem lies within us. I have seen this more often to be the case. It is usually our attitude that brings this on. As they say, we need an attitude adjustment. So, before you lash out at others, take a closer look at yourself. It just might be you that needs to change.

"How are you doing today? Are you okay? Is there anything I can do to help?" The first question is one we most often ask someone when we greet them. We seldom ask the next two questions. The first question is merely a greeting and not a sincere question. The next two show you are genuinely concerned. When greeting people, take notice of them as individuals because the more sensitive you are, the more likely you will know how and when to help. Notice their demeanor, their look, voice, and other telltale signs of stress. Take time to show interest and concern. Be a friend to all.

Exaggerating the truth is lying in another form. People exaggerate when the plain truth doesn't appear to be provocative enough (as one author said, "The lizard claimed to be a dinosaur on his mother's side"). Their agenda is often one-upmanship. These half-truthers wouldn't lie if we didn't condone it. What is it about human nature that causes us to pay any attention to this nonsense? I believe it is our selfish nature – we relish hearing bad things about others, because it makes us feel better about ourselves. Don't lie, don't accept lies, and don't find peace in other people's distortions (especially important in any election year).

"Everyone is wrong but me." We may not admit it, but we often think it. We sometimes get to the point that the world is out of step. This is because things are not going entirely our way. We get discouraged and think the whole world has turned against us. This is a frustrating time for us. It may be a family issue, a medical problem, or an occupation dilemma. Whatever the issue is, it is weighing us down. In these situations, we need to step back, take a deep breath and re-organize ourselves. When we get back our wits and think through our situation, we will undoubtedly come up with a good plan. We just need time to think things through. Things usually turn out for the best. We just need to hang in there.

Recently, during an NBA playoff game with the Cleveland
Cavaliers, Draymond Green of the Golden State Warriors was
suspended for kicking LeBron James of the Cleveland
Cavaliers — in the groin as James was stepping over him. Green
took James stepping over him as a sign of disrespect. Whether it
be sports, politics, religion, or other contests, good
sportsmanship seems to be out the window. Why do we feel the
need to exhibit such poor behavior? In a word: selfishness.
Somehow, we feel we are more important than anyone else. We
hate it when someone disrespects us. Our egos are just too
important to us. Find it in your heart to just let it go. Don't
harbor grudges or animosity. It will just eat you up and make
you a much weaker person.

Let's look at the word "kindness." Most people consider
themselves as being kind to others, so it is an important concept
to understand.

Kindness is defined as a characteristic of ethical behavior, of
loving respect, and a pleasant disposition. So, take a close look
at yourself and ask the following questions: Am I a kindly
individual? Do I have loving respect for others? Unfortunately,
it has been my experience that the majority of our society today
does not have a loving respect for people.

Kindness also requires having a pleasant personality. The
characteristics of having a pleasant personality entail holding
others in even higher esteem than we do ourselves. We are not
judgmental, we do not use condescending language, we harbor
no unkind feelings for others, and we are helpful to others.

The world can use more people with pleasant behavior and a pleasant personality. Join with me and strive to become a more kindly person. This is the best present we can give ourselves, our family, and our country.

It used to be that we conversed primarily by phone and letters. Now we converse more through texts, emails and social media. This has caused us to be more distant with each other on a personal basis. Yes, we see more photos and hear more quickly from each other, but there is something about hearing an actual voice that is reassuring and more personal. It's hard to capture that intimate contact if we rely strictly on texts, tweets, Snapchat, etc. I know people who now won't answer their phone and demand you text them instead. They claim it is to avoid robo and sales calls. However, if we don't pick up the phone or visit with each other, we will lose the art of communication.

When people's minds are made up, they quit listening and start debating. You can tell when someone's mind is already made up (even your own). It is when the first words out of someone's mouth is "I disagree." Game over. Further communication is typically useless, for it is already a debate and not a discussion. Each of us wants to defend our position no matter what. Likewise, they might not even say they disagree, but instead just change the subject or walk away. So, how do you engage someone with a made-up mind to have a discussion? Don't vocalize your disagreement. Start by asking sincere questions to better understand their point of view. Talk in normal tones and avoid raising your voice. Smile a lot and compliment them when they make a good point. Listen more than you talk. Don't repeat or press your point. If you are kind and courteous, you can have a very worthwhile discussion even when you think it started off Balkanized.

There is no justification for wasting time. Your clock is "ticking" and you only have a short while to make your imprint on humanity. You may not have held an important office, or position, or written a book. But you can be of value. You have a family, friends, community. Take care of them, especially family, for they are most important thing you have on this earth.

We can all have disagreements but still be agreeable. Today while I was at a football game, I became engaged with a fellow next to me regarding politics. When there appeared to be a difference in opinion on a particular issue, he said that we had nothing else to talk about. He said it in a rather rude way. In life, we are going to have differences of opinions; but, we can still be agreeable with one another without hurting someone's feelings. In other words, differences in viewpoints should not make us disagreeable. We need to treat each other with dignity and respect, even when we don't agree on certain issues, especially political ones.

We all struggle for attention. It begins when we are an infant and doesn't cease until we have left the Earth. Some struggle in silence, while others yell and scream their head off. It is this struggle for attention that defines who we are. If you are egotistical, you're out there strutting around like a screaming peacock. Most are content to quietly go about their daily routines until something happens that makes them feel the need to be heard. Try and be normal. Then, when you need to be heard, others are more likely to listen.

If I can do just one thing right, let me be a good father and husband. The most important thing to me is my family. All my waking hours are spent on behalf of my family. They are the main reason for my existence. I want to express my appreciation to my good parents who taught me correct principles and gave me a great foundation to start my own family. My father revered my mother, and this has been a main stay for me throughout my nearly 56 years of marriage. Families are forever, and we need to treat them this way. If you are a father, revere your wife, provide adequately for your family, and raise your children with your good example and training. Teach your children the honest principle of hard work. If you are a mother, revere your husband. Provide a peaceful and loving clean home. Teach your children correct principles. The mother is the best teacher. Don't leave this up to the schools. If you are a child, honor your parents. Help around the home. Treat your siblings with respect: don't tease. Make the world a better place by making your family a better place.

Have you ever heard the expression "The best things in life are free"? It means that we don't always have to spend money to enjoy life. So, what are the "best" things in life that are free? Happiness is at the heart of the best things. True happiness comes from serving others: our families, friends, neighbors, and communities. The more time we spend helping others, the more happy and fulfilling our life will be. Truly, the best things in life *are* free … freely given.

What I like about looking at our Earth from space is that I see no borders, no language differences, no conflicts, only a beautiful blue planet. After all, we are all one people, the unique inhabitants of this wonderful world we call home. I liken this to beholding myself in a mirror. When I stand up close, I see the flaws: the wrinkles, the grey hair, and other blemishes. But, when I stand back, I see a normal human being. No wrinkles, no grey hair or blemishes. I think we all should stand back and look at each other this way. When we do, each of us becomes more attractive, less threatening. We forget about our differences. I like this. If I need to get closer, I will just close my eyes and believe I am seeing a wonderful member of my extended Earth family. Will you join me on this journey to have a better view and perspective of our fellow man?

Life

The grizzled old musician Ray Hubbard once said, "The days my gratitude is higher than my expectations, those are really good days." Psychology Professor Robert Emmons amplifies this insight by noting, "Gratitude blocks toxic emotions, such as envy, resentment, regret and depression, which can destroy our happiness... It allows individuals to celebrate the present and be an active participant in their own lives... It focuses the mind on what an individual already has rather than something that's absent..." The fact is, you have much to be grateful for. You are your own boss; you have a vision worth chasing; and you are creating products people want, hiring people who need work, and achieving things quietly desperate people won't. Call it "counting your blessings" if you like, but when you do, you cannot help but be more positive in your outlook, and that makes all inconveniences seem petty.

Let us all press on with a steadfastness in love, being unwavering in our determination to do good continuously. With a world so filled with hatred, we need more of us doing good and being kind toward others. We need to develop the trait of humility. When we are humble, we have more of a propensity to do good continuously.

Life is like a chess game. You must continually be looking ahead. Thinking ahead is just good planning. The better you are at this, the more you're going to get out of your life.

If you live a charmed life, then chances are you just haven't lived long enough.

I have often heard people say, "Life is too short." What they are really saying is: "I really don't need this headache." They are obviously bothered with the challenges they face. These kinds of challenges are usually non-productive ones that have to be dealt with anyway, but are a real pain, like a flat tire or a broken pipe. But this is life. We are going to have headache problems. To this I say, "Aren't you glad you are alive and healthy, so you can do this?" Just smile and get on with it.

Where do we go from here? This is a question we sometimes ask ourselves when we are in a predicament. Life is always going to be fraught with challenges with which we need to cope. We resist change, because it means we have to deal with it. Whether it is a job, marriage, family, health, home, etc., we have to meet it head on. This is both the bane and beauty of life. Life is a wonderful experience if you look at the challenges as an opportunity for growth.

Have you ever pondered why you are here on earth? We all ask ourselves, "Where did I come from and where do I go after life is over?" Stephen Hawking opined that "If we knew the origin and creation of the universe, we would know the mind of God." Man has sought to understand these questions for centuries. Know this. You are not here by accident. You have a purpose. You are unique. There is no one on Earth more important than you. Find your place in this tangle of humanity. Be a force for good. Don't waste the opportunity. Your time on Earth is important. Make the best of it.

Do you have a gold standard for your life? Personal gold standards are life principles held sacred and ones you live by. These standards and principles help guide you in your daily decisions: such as having honesty, integrity, and respect for all people, doing whatever it takes without excuses. If you have these kind of standards, you will be not only successful, but happy.

"Despair" is the complete loss of "hope." It is a feeling we get when things do not appear to be going our way ... a feeling of "helplessness." If you think about this a little, you will soon realize there are only a very few things you can actually determine the outcome of, because most things are not within your direct control. This is where "hope" comes in. Hope keeps us from despair. Hope fosters optimism and it is optimism that keeps hope alive. If you are hopeful, you will be optimistic. Most everyone loves an optimist. So be hopeful and avoid despair.

Are you making a mountain out of a mole hill? This happens when our egos get in the way. This cannot only be costly, it can ruin friendships. Ego is not our friend ... it is usually our enemy. So how do we let our egos get in the way? Rein in our pride, the great destroyer. "Pride precedes the fall." Pride gets in the way of progress. Nothing good ever comes from pride. Pride is haughty, not humble. It can be all-encompassing. Fight pride as though it was your worst enemy.

We were recently in Hawaii and my wife said, "Come look at this beautiful sunset." I was working on something and hesitated a little too long before getting up. A sunset is the most beautiful just as it sinks below the horizon. I felt bad that I missed that moment because I hesitated. In life, timing is everything: a baby's first step, a child's first words, a graduation, a sunset, helping a friend in need, and so many others. Let's not be so preoccupied that we miss out on those beautiful experiences that happen so infrequently.

The world is full of "well wishers." "Hope you're doing well." "Have a nice day." But what we really need are "well helpers." People who don't just wish us well, but rather jump in, without being asked, to lend a helping hand. Action speaks louder than words. God bless these gentle souls that show their love by their deeds, not their words. Talk is cheap. Be a doer, not a talker.

Too many in Silicon Valley strive for riches. This is what's wrong with Silicon Valley. They should strive for wisdom first. With wisdom, they will be better suited to handle wealth, if this is their pursuit. But true riches come from helping others. There is wisdom in this.

Happiness comes from within; "fun" comes from without. Getting happiness from doing fun things is short-lived. True and long-lasting "happiness" comes from doing things for others. Serving others brings us joy that doing fun things cannot. Seeing others succeed can put a smile on our face. Giving a helping hand to someone in need can warm the cockles of our hearts. A word of encouragement to someone in distress can make our burdens seem lighter. "Happiness" is one of the greatest gifts we can give ourselves: but you won't find it at the amusement park.

Want to live a happier life? Find ways to help others. It feels better when you do. The times I recall being the best of my life were those when I have gone out my way to be helpful. Be happy, serve others first.

All problems are not really problems. Many are ones we make up. We create them to make us seem busy or to get sympathy - the "woe is me" syndrome. We have enough real challenges without creating make-believe ones. What are some of these not-real problems? "What should I wear today?" or "What should we have for dinner?" These kinds of non-problems consume our mindshare and distract us from our real challenges. Don't get distracted by trivial issues.

Do the Tough Things First and improve your output. The things that tend to bog us down, and prevent us from getting the most out of our day, are those things which are difficult. We stew about them and in the end put them off until later. In other words, they get delayed. This doesn't mean we stop stewing about them. Oh no! They are on our minds until we tackle them or put them off even further. They never really go away, even though we hope they will. You can get 20% more done every day if you tackle the difficult things first. Get them out of the way and the rest of your day will go better.

When you are having difficulty sleeping, it can often be caused from stress in your life. Instead of tossing and turning and wondering if you will ever get to sleep, try thinking of the blessings you have enjoyed, instead of worrying about those things that are giving you stress. I know this is easier said than done, but once you practice reflecting on the good in your life, you will fall asleep with a smile on your face.

When you abandon your moral values, you abandon your self-respect. We saw this recently in the Olympics when three notable U.S. swimmers lied about an incident in a gas station and tried to cover the incident by blaming it on some Brazilian thugs posing as policemen. This incident will forever haunt them. These kinds of stories are played out in less notable situations every day. Why we abandon our moral values is an interesting study in human behavior. It is all about greed. One of the worst characteristics we can have. The reward of this evil characteristic is fleeting at best. Greed has no lasting value. It raises its hideous head whenever we feel those debase lusts or desires. Abandoning our moral values, ultimately leads to self-destruction. If you truly love yourself and your loved ones, hold to those moral values like you would your own life, because in the end the end, it could cost you your life.

Lovemaking has long been considered sexual relations between individuals. This is not really love. Love is defined as the very intense feeling of affection towards another: like a mother feels for her child. She would protect the child, even with her life. Love is giving one's all for another. It is filled with joy or sorrow. It has no bounds or limitations. It is all-encompassing. It is not fleeting, but eternal. This is real "love."

The most costly mistake we can make is not admitting we've made a mistake. The reason for this is threefold. First, by not admitting the mistake, there will be no correction. Second, the damage caused will not be repaired. Third, we will not learn from the mistake, and it most likely will be repeated. This perpetuates the mistake and the damages will continue. While admitting we made a mistake goes against our nature, not admitting we made a mistake will, in the long run, be our undoing.

As we ponder our future, we need to think about where we want to be five years from now. We need to ask: "Is where I am now going to get me where I want to be in five years?" The future is just around the corner and happens faster than we think. Our life is so precious that we need to put a great deal of thought and preparation into it. If we don't plan our life, someone else will. Take control of your life. Don't let someone else do it for you.

It is never too late to say:

- I am sorry.
- I love you.
- I forgive you.
- How can I help you?
- You are the best.
- Thanks for being my friend.
- Thanks for all you do.

These are but a few of the words of kindness that will bring joy and happiness to those you come in contact with.

I was talking with a friend of mine recently and I asked him how his day had been. "Not too good," he exclaimed. "My wife may have cancer." I asked him how he felt. His answer surprised me. I thought he might say, "I am really worried," or "I am really bummed out." Instead, he said, "Well, that's the way it goes." His comment is not unusual. Life is full of ups and downs. In other words, there is no value or need to pine about it. We just have to deal with it. He has the right attitude. We all are going to have to face very difficult trials. This is life. Let's move on. Hope for the best, but be prepared for the worst.

Be a winner by being a willing listener and serving others before yourself.

The truth about who you are is defined by how you live your life and how you are perceived by others. What kind of example do you set? This would be the way in which you touch and affect other people's lives. You can measure this by seeing how others react when they are around you. Do they seem comfortable? Are they anxious to hear what you have to say? Are you a willing listener? Do you openly praise others? Are you a happy and optimistic person? Ask your closest friend to rate you on how you are perceived by others. You will be surprised by the answers you get.

If you want to ensure your success, I have a sure-fire way for you to do this. Approach your plan as though your life depends on a successful outcome. In other words, pretend that you have only one shot at making it successful. Taking this view will help you be more careful and thoughtful about your plan.

If you are bored or otherwise unhappy in your job, you need to rethink how you view your employment. Two options exist: One, talk to your supervisor about the job and work out a possible change or modification to your work. Second, look for another job. Neither you nor the company are benefiting if you are unhappy. Don't feel caught in a no-win situation. Do something about it.

Life is full of twists and turns. We will be bent and shaped by our life experiences. If we are well-rooted, with solid values, the ups and downs and those twists and turns will not uproot us, no matter how challenging our trails may be.

"I don't have a choice, or do I?" Sometimes we are caught on the horns of a dilemma. It appears we don't have a choice. An example I give in my book "Tough Things First" was when I attended college and decided to quit school. My father gave me a choice: go back to school or give up everything I had acquired up to that point, like my car and clothes (walk away into the world naked). To me, that was no choice at all. In real life, choices are rarely easy. We have choices, but not all alternatives are palatable. It is the proverbial "darned if we do and darned if we don't," the choosing of the lesser of the two evils. No matter how distasteful the alternatives are, we must decide ... and decide we will or suffer the consequences because indecision has a price.

We normally think of spring cleaning as what we do around the house. I also think of spring cleaning as something that I need to do with myself. Am I optimistic, happy, helpful, healthy, patient, kind, and charitable? I am always looking for ways to improve, and spring is good time to take personal inventory. How about you? Ready for some personal spring cleaning?

What ever happened to the phrase, "You have my word"? We once used the phrase all the time, with the dignity that comes from a sense of honor. Now it is more of a cliché, with too many people willing to cross their fingers behind their backs. We need to add that word "honor" as in, "You have my word of honor." When your honor is on the line, it becomes tough to renege on a pledge. Be a person of your word by being a person of honor.

I was talking with someone this week who said that they were operating in stealth mode. So, what really is stealth mode, and how can we apply it in our daily life? In the military sense, stealth mode is operating undetected. In other words, the enemy knows you're coming but they can't see you or don't know you're there. We need to consider operating more in stealth mode, so that we don't always bring attention to ourselves. Try stealth mode in your life by doing good things without needing to be noticed.

When looking for a job, are you looking for money or an opportunity? Most employers will soon find out. If your focus is money, your chances are worse in landing the job. Employers are looking for loyalty, and thus focus on your job history. If you have changed jobs on an average of three years or less, this will not portray you as a loyal employee. Employers are looking for dedicated team members who have a track record of dependability.

The worth of something is highly dependent on the view each of us places on its importance. If the item is of little or no importance to us, we assign little or no value to it. On the other hand, if the item is important, we will assign whatever value it takes to acquire it. Apply this thinking to a relationship. If the relationship is of little importance to us, we do little to maintain it. But if the person is an important part of our lives, we work diligently to preserve it. Ergo, if your job – which is a relationship – is important to you, you must work as hard as necessary to retain it.

The challenge is the challenge. We are all up for a good challenge, but how about a bad challenge? We dread the bad challenges! But let's face it – we are going to have bad challenges, at least as we see it. So, let's change a bad challenge into a good challenge. You ask, "How can we do that?" It isn't easy, but it can be done. Usually a bad challenge is not of our choosing. We just have to maintain the view that we are going to make the best of it. We are going to turn lemons into lemonade.

I want your help ... if it is the help I want. There is often a gap between the help we want versus the help others are willing to give us. In most cases, the help we want is to have someone take care of a problem we face. For example, provide an answer to a problem rather than showing us how to solve it ourselves. Some might say it is the difference between giving someone a fish and showing them how to fish. The latter is better. The real help we should seek is learning and knowledge, not just someone bailing us out.

If you are going to gamble, and I don't believe in gambling, make sure you bet on the right horse. To gamble is to make a serious bet on some outcome. So how can it be called gambling if you bet on the right horse? "Right" horse in this case doesn't mean you know the horse will win. The "right" horse, in this instance, is a worthwhile gamble, such as a career, marriage, business venture, an investment or the like. Avoid games of chance such as the roulette wheel, risky ventures, or the like. Any form of gambling should be done with careful thought and study.

"I can't win for losing." This expression sums up how many people feel about their lives. So, what is losing really? In most cases, it refers to us not getting what we want when we want it. Having everything we want when we want it is not only unrealistic, it would be awfully boring. We would not know the sweet unless we taste the bitter. We would not feel joy, unless we've experienced failure. As the other saying goes, "Variety is the spice of life." We need to lose occasionally to truly savor a win. Therefore, you do win by losing.

Some regard meekness as weakness. But true meekness implies a spirit of gratitude, as opposed to an attitude of self-sufficiency, an acknowledgment of a greater power beyond oneself. It is the recognition of our need and dependency on others. In this sense, meekness is really a strength: a strength of character. It is inherent in being humble. Humility is one of the greatest characteristics that we can have. Inculcated in the characteristics of humility and meekness is, of course, gratitude. If we could all learn to be more grateful, what a better world we would have.

When looking for a new job, make sure there is a cultural fit between you and the new company - a thorough investigation is in order. If you have acquaintances at the new company, get valuable insights from them about how they and you fit the corporate culture. This is especially important today given the wide variety of age groups in various companies. If it is an older, well-established company, the average age will likely be higher. If it is a newer, high-tech company, the age makeup will be younger. In any case, the age makeup and social majority will affect the culture. You need to understand these various demographics, since they could have an impact on your future.

Sometimes, the world we live in is referred to as "the cold, cruel world." At times, it can appear that way.

All of us face many challenges and adversities, and it is natural that we can get depressed. Life can get pretty difficult. We may even say to ourselves, "Oh, to heck with everything."

However, when we step back and look at all this realistically, we see that if we never had any bad times, we would never know what good times are like. We learn though overcoming challenges and difficulties. We might never learn without adversity, and if we never learn, we never progress.

Therefore, this so-called cold, cruel world is just what we need. To this I say, "Come what may and love it." Just keep a stiff upper lip and "keep on truckin'." It is all for our good and development.

None of us like to point fingers. So why do we do it? Is it because we don't want to take responsibility? Or, is it we don't want to get blamed for a screw-up? In either case, pointing fingers means we are selfish. Now, none of us would ever want to admit we are selfish, would we? Well, think back at the last time you pointed a finger. Weren't you trying to avoid something? This is just another way of being selfish. The next time you feel the urge to point a finger, just put your finger between your teeth first and bite down.

When I am not busy, I feel worthless. Have you felt this way? Being engaged in a worthy cause is what life is all about. Finding and staying engaged in those worthy causes, though, is not easy. It takes careful and consistent planning. But to get the most out of life, we need to give back in a consistent manner. If in doubt, find some worthy cause to get involved with.

The world tries to change our behavior by changing our environment. This is an outside-in approach, and it is a hopeless cause. The only way to change behavior is by each of us, as individuals, changing our nature. This is an inside-out approach and is the only way we truly change.

What will be your legacy? How will you be remembered? It takes a lifetime to build a legacy, but only a few misdeeds to destroy it. Take for example, Olympic swimming star, Ryan Lochte. He was a gold medalist at the recent Olympics. However, one dishonest deed has now severely tarnished his legacy. It takes a long time and hard work to build a great reputation, but only a few seconds to kill it. Keep your legacy alive and well. Don't let anything or anyone harm it. Guard it with your life, because it *is* your life.

Stumbling blocks are there to help us progress, not to fail. As difficult as it may appear, and as uncomfortable as it makes us feel, these challenges are actually what we need to take us to the next level. Rather than cursing these setbacks, we should actually be thankful for them.

Staying above the fray is like flying above the clouds. On our way back from a recent trip, we were far above a massive storm that was heading for our destination. At 33,000 feet, the air was smooth. But we knew that eventually we would descend through the thunder, with its white-knuckle turbulence. So, it is with life. We can stay above life's clouds for so long; then, we have to face them. We have to buckle up and ride it out.

You can't define your own truth. While perception may become our own reality, it is not necessarily the truth. Sometimes, when we lie often enough, it becomes a truth to us. If you can't be honest with yourself, you will not be honest with others. Truth is truth; don't define your own.

When we refer to someone as having strength of character, we mean that they have high integrity. High integrity means that in every case, and in all instances, they do the right thing. They don't worry if their emails fall into the wrong hands or get hacked. "If you always tell the truth, you don't need to have a good memory." I would add, "If you have high integrity, you don't have to worry about what bad things people may find out about you in the future." Live your life as if you live in a fish bowl. You can never go wrong doing what's right.

I am intrigued with rhetoric surrounding the term "fake" news. The word "fake" means: not genuine. Genuine means to be authentic, completely honest. When we color words and concepts to make them appear like we want, as opposed to what they really are, it is a "fake." It is like taking a circle of lead painted the color of gold and calling it a gold ring. Yes, the ring is gold-looking but when we try to pass it off as authentic gilt, we are being blatantly dishonest. Twisting what others are saying to force another conclusion is also being dishonest or "fake." Not telling the whole truth by leaving out certain critical pieces of information is being dishonest and "fake." When testifying, we promise to tell the whole truth and nothing but the truth. And if we do not, we can be held in contempt and imprisoned. We should always conduct ourselves in a manner where we are always being totally honest. We should never want anyone to think of us as "fake."

❃ ❃ ❃

I was listening to our piano tuner tune our piano today and was amazed at how he can stand to do such a repetitive task and enjoy it. He said something interesting that I had not thought of before. What I considered to be boring and mundane were the most interesting and challenging aspects to him. I heard only a repetitive banging away on the piano, but he hears many dimensions because he is an artist and this is his trade. This is true in many occupations that seem boring and mundane because we don't appreciate the art. We need to appreciate the art involved in all occupations before we judge them.

Many of us think we can win in life without knowing the rules. Those rules are found in the New Testament's Book of Matthew:

- Blessed are the poor in spirit, meaning not haughty.

- Blessed are those who mourn; they are compassionate.

- Blessed are the meek, which means being humble.

- Blessed are those who hunger and thirst for righteousness.

- Blessed are the merciful; this means those that do not condemn or judge.

- Blessed are the pure in heart, who are honest and have integrity.

- Blessed are the peacemakers.

- Blessed are those who are persecuted for righteousness sake.

You might consider these rules as you look at yourself.

We have all heard the term "He is down on his luck." This refers to someone who is not doing very well. This might involve financial problems, health issues, loss of a loved one, spouse issues, issues with children, loss of a job, or many other misfortunes. No matter what the issue may be, it is dire to the person undergoing the problem. This is where we can help. We all know someone who is going through hard times. Let's be sensitive to those individuals and lend encouragement, a helping hand, prayers, a listening ear … whatever it takes. Be a friend, a good friend.

Is it ever too late? Sometimes, but not always. This is what I call having "no regrets." To have "no regrets", we need to be aware of all issues, both big and small, that impact our lives. It is when we ignore these issues, in the hopes they will resolve themselves, that we end up with the proverbial "regrets." It is a dangerous and foolish notion that most issues resolve themselves. The saying "Time heals all wounds," has some truth; but, it is not the same way to have "no regrets." It is usually our egos that get in the way of us dealing with these difficult issues. This is one area in which you don't want to procrastinate. Just like leaving a physical wound untreated is not wise, leaving a psychological wound untreated can be just as dangerous. Treat it now, and it will never be too late. And, you will have "no regrets."

With power comes responsibility — the responsibility to look out for others. Be a valued mentor. There are those among us who need our help. They may be our neighbors, a family member, a member of the community/nation. As the Scout motto tells us: "Do a good turn daily."

Because I no longer run a big company, I am asked how I like retirement. When I was working full-time, I dreaded the thought of not working or, as some have called it, retirement. I have a good friend who retired some years ago and every time I call him to check on how he is doing, he is always baby-sitting his grandkids. Now don't get me wrong, bonding with grandkids is a good thing, but not as a full-time job. In any case, I vowed that if ever stopped working full-time, I would stay busy and not sit on a rock in Hawaii. I still have my usual routine. I get up at 5:30 a.m., exercise, shower, get dressed in slacks and a dress shirt, eat, and then go to work on my book marketing and mentoring startups. I am as busy as I was when I was working full-time. This is my idea of how to avoid getting rusty in retirement.

Over the span of your career, you will find that not all of your bosses are good. But keep in mind, nothing good can come from mean-mouthing a bad boss. During the interview process, people who bad-mouth their boss are not perceived as good candidates. The point is, you can be looking for a new job without insulting the previous company or manager. When interviewing with a new company, focus on why you want to come to the new company, not why you are leaving the old one.

Who knows? That bad boss may someday be a great reference for you.

Have you found your niche in life? Every one of us has a special niche. What is yours? It's like looking for buried treasure. Find your niche, because that is where your gold is. A niche is a specialized position in life or employment. Whether you believe it or not, you are better at something than anyone else. You do have a special talent. This does make you unique. The challenge, for all of us, is to find that special talent that is uniquely ours. My suggestion is to ask others what they think your talents are. Most people who know you well will freely offer their opinions. Make a list of these and work to develop them. Then you will be on your way to make your unique mark on society.

Reporters and interviewers constantly ask me, "What are you doing in retirement?" I'm working harder than ever. My mother, who was a schoolteacher until her mid-seventies, had a mind sharper than tacks. But upon retirement, she just sat around and watched TV. It wasn't long before she began to develop dementia. If you're going to retire, and if you want to maintain your mental acuity, you better keep your mind busy.

Are we at peace with ourselves? This means that we are happy in the face of all our trials. We don't look at our trials as a burden, but rather as an opportunity for growth. Happiness comes from the reassurance that the adversities we face will, in time, be resolved.

Why is it so hard to admit when we are wrong? It has to do with change, which people dislike in general. Admitting we are wrong requires us to change our minds. So, the real question should be is: Why is it so hard for us to accept such change? The answer is complicated, since the mind works differently for each situation and person. The most common response among all people is that once we have decided something, we don't want to think about it anymore. We think: "Don't confuse me with the facts; my mind is made up already." It takes time, patience, and empathy to change someone's mind, especially your own.

Ⓨ Ⓨ Ⓨ

A stranger was moving behind my friend's vehicle and tripped over the trailer hitch that extended out a little behind. This stranger waited until my friend returned to give him a piece of his mind for having a trailer hitch that stuck out the way most hitches do. My friend felt awful and embarrassed, mainly due to the loud outburst of rage from the stranger. My friend apologized and asked the stranger if he was hurt (he wasn't, he was merely annoyed). My friend wondered why the stranger was so quick to blame someone other than himself for not being more careful. It is a sad fact that in our world today, we look for others to blame, rather than looking at ourselves first. Did my friend have culpability in this incident? Yes, but so did the stranger. We should not be so quick to judge. Angry outbursts are not a good way to resolve our differences.

Ⓨ Ⓨ Ⓨ

Each of us builds our lives day by day. This is our "bucket" that we fill with good deeds and effort. When we do something wrong or don't put forth our best effort, we punch holes in our bucket and lose the good contents we have worked so hard for. These holes make it more difficult for us to refill our life's bucket. It requires a great deal of extra effort until we plug the leaks. Patching our buckets requires making amends for the wrongs we have done or exerting extra effort to compensate for less than robust past performance. If you want to be more productive and get more out of your life, don't punch holes in your life's bucket, and don't punch holes in other people's buckets either.

No matter how much we pray, no matter how hard we try, bad things are going to happen to good people. This is just the way it is. As the saying goes, "It rains on the good and the bad". An acquaintance of mine lost his job a year ago and, just today, his wife lost her job too. They are demoralized and defeated. We all have been praying for rain here in California because of the drought, but now many of my friends are getting flooded out and are experiencing significant damage to their homes. If you are not experiencing some hardships and difficulties, you are either dead or unusually lucky. When I experience difficulties, I remind myself to just wait because good times are just around the corner and sure enough, they come. There is a saying I like that goes, "Come what may and love it." Having this perspective helps you to be happy regardless of transient circumstances.

Can you be true to yourself if you are not doing your best? Look back over your performance last week. Can you say you did your best? I like to take a weekly stock of how I did that week and find ways I can improve. It is all about being true to myself. I want to do better. How about you?

We all know that stress can be a killer. So how can we deal with stress? One approach is to learn how to love the things you hate. Studies show that the kind of stress that is harmful to us is when we are doing things we don't like doing. So, one way to deal with stressful things is to learn to love those things we don't like doing. As the saying goes, "If you love your work, you won't work a day in your life." So, the key to relieving stress is to love the things you detest doing.

To misstate the truth, whether it be about reality or non-reality, is a "lie." Once you begin to deceive, a complex web you begin to weave. Your misdeeds and lies will come back to haunt you all the days of your life. Honesty and integrity are at the heart of being truthful. Being completely truthful, whether it will hurt you or not, is the only way to have a truly happy life.

"Come what may and love it." This is a saying I heard, a few years ago, from a very thoughtful leader. It speaks to my heart because it has the message that if we take all things that happen to us in stride, we will be happier and more optimistic. My sister is going through cancer treatments, and it is extremely difficult for her. She asks, "Why me? Do I need to learn something? Am I being punished for something I did?" These are all natural feelings when it seems the world is collapsing around us. It is very difficult to be happy when bad things are happening to us. But being angry and upset does not improve the situation. In fact, it may prevent or at least slow down the healing process. Studies show that a happy attitude actually helps healing. If you are going through difficult times, try being happy and improve the healing process.

The clock is ticking, but we don't hear it. Why? Because we are so caught up in the moment. Most of us live in the present or dwell on the past. We are taught to slow down and smell the roses. But the clock is ticking, and before we know, it we ask ourselves: "Where has the time gone, and it just seemed like yesterday?" This is what happens when we don't look ahead toward the future. If we don't plan for the future, we will not be ready for it. Yes, live life to the fullest and get the most out of each day. However, give some thought about tomorrow, because tomorrow is yesterday today.

Rainbows come and go. These represent the inevitable peaks and valleys of mortality. We all face them. The main difference is how we deal with them. Sometimes we laugh, and sometimes we cry. Some take these ups and down in stride, while others bemoan their very existence. We all love it when life is going wonderfully, but that is not how things are going to be forever. So, when blackbirds come and the rainbow disappears, just remember that soon the bluebirds and rainbows will return.

Some claim to be a victim of their circumstances. In truth, they are a victim of their decisions. Our lives are the sum of all our decisions. We all have the freedom of choice. Choose wisely.

As hard as I try not to make mistakes, they still occur even when I am sensitive to the possibility. For example, when I send emails, I read and re-read them before I hit the send button. Even with this diligence, I still make errors from time to time. The reason for this is that I wrote the text, and when I re-read it, my mind passes over obvious errors. This also applies when you communicate verbally. Occasionally, someone will take what I said the wrong way because of how I said it. This causes me to ask myself, "Did I really say that?" I check to discover if I have been misinterpreted, or if I said it wrong. It's a good policy to assume you may have made a mistake, rather than assume others did. This can be tough because our egos get in the way. Just remember, whether you are communicating in writing or verbally, it is your responsibility to make your message clear.

We never know how long we will live. A friend of mine recently passed away. It was a shock to all of us. He was a fitness buff and was always conscious of his health. While we are saddened by his untimely death, we should keep in mind those he left behind. They are the ones that are going to bear the loss. Life is precious and should not be wasted on trivial pursuits. Make the most of your time here on Earth, for you never know when it will end.

Dealing with the inevitable takes courage and understanding. The inescapable will happen, no matter how much we wish it wouldn't. It is part of the cycle we face in life. Amidst the sunshine in our lives, we confront challenges and adversities. Dealing with these effectively requires us to anticipate and be prepared for them. Having a good savings account, health insurance, and the proper perspective helps to deal with the inevitable. Don't be afraid of these dark periods. Just know that following every storm is the bright sunshine. "And these things too shall pass."

Sometimes, the wrong road is the right road. "How can that be?" you ask. It is because we don't always make the right decisions. After all, we are human and don't have perfect knowledge. We believe the road we are on is the "right" road, or we would not have taken it. However, because of our inability to make perfect decisions, the "right" road (the one we are on) could be the wrong road. Ironically then, the "wrong" road might actually be the "right" road. So, what's the purpose of all this double-talk? Simply this: be willing to question the road you are on. You might be on the wrong road, even though you think it is right one.

They say that: "The only sure things in life are death and taxes." We live with the certainty that almost everything in life is uncertain. This is what makes our lives so interesting. It is like opening up a present every day. I just love the saying: "Yesterday is history, tomorrow is a mystery, but today is the present and that's why they call it a gift." You can't change the past or the future. You can only change the present. Each day is a gift that we should cherish. Make the most of today, and tomorrow will take care of itself.

❂   ❂   ❂

If you are fighting for survival, you probably didn't have a good plan to survive. Plan ahead.

❂   ❂   ❂

The greatest achievements we can make in life come through personal sacrifice. It is when we put it all on the line and have given it all we have. Then, and only then, will we feel truly fulfilled. When we retire at night and look back over our day, we should ask ourselves, "What good have I done in the world today. Have I helped anyone in need?" Resolve to reach out and help others. If you do, your life will become more meaningful and fulfilled.

❂   ❂   ❂

I recently did an interview for a news organization. The theme of the interview was: *What I Learned from the Mistakes I Made*. It was to be somewhat self-deprecating. It is difficult to make fun of ourselves, especially because of costly mistakes. How honest will we be? This question went through my mind as I prepared for the interview (I had no problem with incidents that were minor, but the interviewer wanted juicier examples). Preparing for the interview was of the most value. It caused me to seriously reflect on my past 37 years of running my company. I was not perfect and did make some stupid mistakes. The issue is, did I learn from the mistakes? I can honestly say I made lots of different mistakes and did not repeat them. Learning does not prevent us from making new mistakes. We are not perfect, and we will continue to make stupid—yet different—mistakes and continue to learn and grow.

Some of us are literally fighting for our lives. It consumes all our mind share. Our health is our most important asset, along with our time. Health issues can distract us and should distract us from doing other things. Others, who are aware of this, should be considerate of those people dealing with serious health issues. We are all part of the larger human family. Let's help and support one another. Who knows when it will be our turn to need help?

Holding a grudge, harboring bad feelings or hatred toward someone, cankers our soul. Left unchecked, this can permanently stymie our progress.

Why? Because these kinds of feelings preoccupy us, devour our time, attention and patience, and thus spiral us downward. Do not take harboring hard feelings lightly, as if it is a normal thing. It may be normal in that other people succumb to this hideous problem, but make no mistake about it, it can ruin your life.

Hard feelings can come quickly and are hard to correct. For this reason, we need to corral grudges before they take root.

In books, the classics are largely tragedies. So why the fixation on tragedy? I think this is because we like to know we are not the only ones to face difficulties. "Misery loves company." It is interesting that tragedy makes a longer impression on us than success. Tragedy stimulates more emotion than success. In a way, this is good, since we continue to strive for success and not for tragedy. Emotion related to tragedy is so emphatic that it can drive us into deep depression. Just like when we are deathly ill, we wonder if we are ever going to recover. Thank goodness tragedy doesn't strike every day. To deal with tragedy, we need others to buoy us up. We need our friends and family. The good news with tragedies is that, more often than not, we overcome them. It just takes time and lots of hugs.

We are instruments in directing our lives and the lives of others.

Think of yourself as an important instrument used in navigating an airplane. If this instrument is faulty, it can plunge you and others into disaster. Likewise, if the instrument is good and working properly, it will allow you to safely guide everyone through life.

Leading ourselves astray is one thing, because it will only hurt us. However, it is unlikely we will be the only ones harmed by our poor decisions. More often than not, when we lead ourselves astray, others are hurt in the process.

We can be an instrument for good or evil. It is our choice to be well-calibrated instruments.

Why are we so disagreeable and harsh with each other? This animosity seems to be getting worse. We seem to feel that everyone is out to get us. What ever happened to "love your neighbor"? Part of this increase in hostility stems from media overload. We have instantaneous information access from every corner of the earth. The more negative information we hear causes us to be more negative. We literally carry instant information access in our pockets. So, how can we combat this

and reduce our negativity? Turn off those devices! If you do,
you will find your spirits lifted. You will be more kind and
understanding of your fellow man. Try to live without staying
so tethered.

Gratefulness and entitlement don't seem to go together,
although they should. We are all entitled to be happy, but are
we? We can be happy once we decide to be. Yet, when we have
an entitlement mentality, we cease to be gracious, kind and
happy. Anger stirs us when we don't get what we want, when
we want it. Anger and happiness don't go together. To avoid
the entitlement unhappiness spiral, think back on all those times
when things did go your way. This counting of blessings,
instead of cursing at the world around you, allows you to be
happy, grateful and enjoy life.

Are you "trustworthy"? Meaning, are you worthy of trust from
others? To be trusted is a dignified and valued characteristic. It
has to be earned. You can ask for it, but it will have no meaning
or value until you have proven yourself. Here are some ways
you can earn trust: Be willing to go the extra mile. Be on time to
meetings. Meet all your commitments on time or ahead of
schedule. Be always truthful. Be available to help others. Have a
kindly look. Smile. Be a good listener. Think of others before
yourself. Bottom line: be a good person.

When right is right and wrong is wrong, in your heart you
know it. If you still are not sure, then ask yourself if you would
be proud to admit to what you are about to do to your God.

❧   ❧   ❧

There is a relatively new term called "toxic perfectionism." It refers to a behavioral disorder manifested by an obsessive focus on perfectionism. In my view, this is only dangerous if it results in depression or a loss of self-esteem. Otherwise, the focus on trying to be the best we can, is a good thing.

Being human brings with it certain limitations. For example, we cannot make perfect decisions because to do so, requires us to have a perfect knowledge of the outcome of our decisions. This is not possible because we cannot, with perfect knowledge, know the future.

However, we can act with an almost perfect ability to handle things in the present. I know this sounds confusing because we cannot measure our level of perfection in the present. These measurements can only be viewed in retrospect—like in making bread. As they say, the proof is in the outcome.

To act almost perfectly in the present requires us to know how to perform the task. As Emerson said, "That which we persist in doing becomes easier, not that the nature of the task has changed, but our ability to perform the task has improved."

So here is the clue to acting perfectly in the present. That clue is: "If at first you don't succeed, try, try again." This is how I mean you can act perfectly or strive for perfection. I say that "toxic perfectionism" is:

> 1) expecting perfection without the requisite effort
>
> 2) expecting results that requires knowledge of the future, or

3) expecting unrealistic results, given the conditions being faced

There is everything to be gained by striving for perfection.

Getting the most out of life requires soul searching and planning. The shortcut in this soul searching is to ask yourself, "What is my legacy?" If you died tomorrow, what would you be most remembered for? If the current answer to that question is not pleasing, know that it is not too late to change. In a sense, your legacy is your eternal brand. The most valued and revered aspects of any brand are quality and service. Whether you are an individual contributor, a corporate leader, or a parent, being remembered for good quality and service is something to be sought after. Build a great brand; provide others good value with quality and dedicated service.

"Fearless" honesty is the willingness to tell the truth, regardless of the consequences. It is a rare trait in our society today.

We have been hearing a lot about this on the news media recently, where politicians and high-profile individuals have been struggling with fearless honesty. Any time there are significant consequences, fearless honesty becomes an issue.

Whether it is a high-profile politician, individual, or any of us for that matter, total and unequivocal honesty defines our character. It is not just a matter of being fearlessly honest about a misdeed we have done. Not doing it in the first place is the only way to be totally honest with others and ourselves.

Be totally honest and forthright in all your dealings and you will have no need to worry about the consequences.

Could have, would have, should have. You cannot get to the end of an election cycle without the pundits second-guessing what the candidates could have, would have, should have done. We all, to some degree, do this when we fear the outcome isn't personally desirable. This helps prepare us if the actual outcome isn't what we want. This is Saturday morning quarterbacking for the Sunday game. Hope should spring eternal. We should not give up hope, especially before the outcome is determined.

We can't do much about our physical beauty, but we can alter our emotional attractiveness at will. You can appeal to others even more if you choose to give of yourself, provide encouragement, and let others shine in the spotlight. Outward faults disappear behind inward beauty. Outward attractiveness may fade over time, but inward beauty can continue to grow.

As I sit here writing my book, I hear an awful, grinding noise next door, as my neighbor uses a shredder to mulch tree limbs. It is very distracting and driving me nuts, but I know that work is being performed. While I do not like it, my neighbor seems to. Things are going to happen that disturb and distract us. But, we have to deal with it. Putting up with distractions, from time to time, is just the way life is.

We need to learn to live together in love. Expressing our own opinions is good, as long as it is done in a loving way. When we seek to express our opinions in a way that causes more divisiveness, such as civil disobedience and other contentious ways, it does not help us live together in love. Divisiveness just brings on more divisiveness and moves us further apart. We need to learn to promote our differences in a more loving and positive way. Then, and only then, can we begin to live together in love.

What is the best motivator, love or fear? Throughout history, fear has unfortunately been quite effective for short-term gains. Watch any election cycle.

We can all recall "Dante's Inferno." Dante depicted a horrible place called "Hell," a place we were destined to occupy if we weren't behaving ourselves. I was told as a child, that if I wasn't a good boy, that for Christmas, Santa would leave me a lump of coal in my stocking instead of a toy.

It may be true that "fear" will motivate us for a brief period, but motivating with "love" will have a much longer and positive impact on our behavior. This long-term effect is important when a situation needs correcting. The best approach is to use love, in a timely manner, with gentleness and extreme clarity. Don't try to mince words and wander all over the place in getting to the issue. Be crystal clear, using examples if necessary, in a firm but gentle way. Being angry, condemning, and shouting only worsens the situation. In this case, the recipient is more focused on the diatribe than they are on what needs fixing.

Being calm, collected, and in control will provide far better and longer lasting results. "Love" is the better motivator, and you will be the happier for it. It cuts both ways. Just think how you would feel if the shoe were on the other foot.

I was once engaged in a game of tug-of-war. When we began losing ground, I yelled to my teammates, "Come on guys, pull!" They yelled back, "You need to pull, too!" When we lost, we accused one another of not giving it our best. When things are going fine, we seldom look around for someone to blame, but oh boy, if we are losing, we definitely think someone else failed to pull their weight. It is always someone else and not us!

Have you ever said, "Trust me, I have all the time in the world"? Think about the times you have said this. You really didn't mean it, but you were trying to get a point across that you weren't going to move until you got what you wanted. You are impatient. You have had it up to here. You are upset. So, why do we say this or think this? It's because we are tired of waiting. It is very, very difficult to be a patient "waiter," even though there is a saying that goes, "Good things come to those who wait." "Waiting" is not one of our more sought-after human traits. I think "waiting" is one of the most difficult challenges we face. We want it now, and we hop from one foot to the other until we get it. A super New Year's resolution could be to develop patience. Become a good "waiter."

I have pondered the many human characteristics that I admire:

- Faith
- Hope
- Charity
- Honesty
- Humility
- Integrity
- Diligence
- Vigilance
- Temperance
- Courage
- Kindness

All of these traits are fantastic, and we should seek after them diligently. But, at this time in our history, one stands out as the most redeeming of all: *Kindness*. Oh, we so need more kindness.

A farmer does both planting and harvesting. If you do no planting and only harvesting, then you are primarily a taker and not a giver. We see this in our society where too many of us are taking from the system and not putting anything back. This is a negative sum program. Somehow, we believe the world owes us because we are underprivileged in some way. This thinking is not limited to just people who are on government assistance, but to anyone focused primarily on themselves. They are too fixated on getting what is, in their mind, their "fair share." Be a planter as well as a harvester. Do more giving and less taking, and you'll have a bumper crop of good fortune.

"What have I done with my life?" If you have ever made this comment or had such feelings, you have regrets. Regrets are the bane of mankind, because they haunt us. "If only I had known, I would have done things differently." "Where has the time gone?" But these are useless thoughts for as long as you still have life and will within. The only regret you should have is not making the most out of today.

Take control of your future and not let it take control of you. If we sit back and just let the world go around, it will still go around, and you will be just on for the ride. Wake up and do something now, rather than dreaming of your future. All of us should view our life as an important contribution to the world and not view the world as owing us something. Make your time on earth count for something. Be a faithful contributor, not a relentless taker.

About Ray Zinn

Raymond D. "Ray" Zinn is an inventor, entrepreneur, and the longest serving CEO of a publicly traded company in Silicon Valley.

Zinn is known best for conceptualizing and in effect inventing the Wafer Stepper, and for co-founding semiconductor company Micrel (acquired by Microchip in 2015), which provides essential components for smartphones, consumer electronics and enterprise networks. He has served as Chief Executive Officer, Chairman of its Board of Directors and President since the Company's inception in 1978.

Zinn led Micrel profitably through eight major downturns in global chip markets, an impressive achievement. Many chip companies weren't able to make it through one downturn and very few have survived through all the major downturns. Micrel has been profitable from its very first year, aside from one year during the dot-com implosion.

Ray Zinn holds over 20 patents for semiconductor design. He has been mentioned in several books, including Jim Fixx's *The Complete Book of Running* and *Essentialism* by Greg McKeown.

CPSIA information can be obtained
at www.ICGtesting.com
Printed in the USA
FSHW02n0231020518
47506FS